IRELAND

From the Act of Union • 1800 to the Death of Parnell • 1891

Seventy-seven novels and collections of shorter stories by twenty-two Irish and Anglo-Irish novelists

selected by

PROFESSOR ROBERT LEE WOLFF
Harvard University

A GARLAND SERIES

Laurence Bloomfield
in Ireland

William Allingham

with an introduction by
Robert Lee Wolff

Garland Publishing, Inc., New York & London
1979

For a complete list of the titles in this series,
see the final pages of this volume.

This facsimile has been made from a copy in
the Yale University Library (Ip.A155.864).

The volumes in this series are printed on acid-free,
250-year-life paper.

Library of Congress Cataloging in Publication Data

Allingham, William, 1824–1889.
Laurence Bloomfield in Ireland.

(Ireland, from the Act of Union, 1800,
to the death of Parnell, 1891 ; no. 61)
Reprint of the 1864 ed. published by Macmillan London.
Includes bibliographical references.
1. Ireland—Social life and customs—Poetry.
I. Title. II. Series.
[PR4004.A5A65   1979]   821'.8   78-21980
ISBN 0-8240-3510-0

Printed in the United States of America

Laurence Bloomfield in Ireland
by William Allingham (1824–1889)

Born into a Protestant family in Ballyshannon, Donegal, William Allingham[1] was the son of the town bank manager. Allingham himself went to work at the bank at the age of thirteen, and nine years later, at twenty-two, he entered the customs service and was assigned to various Ulster towns. Having begun to write verse in the early 1840's, he soon made the first of many visits to London, where—initially through Leigh Hunt—he came to know Carlyle, Tennyson, Browning, and the pre-Raphaelites. They liked him and admired his poetry, of which the first collection—*Poems*—appeared in 1850, dedicated to Leigh Hunt. Other volumes of his own verse and anthologies of verse by others—including Edgar Allan Poe—followed at intervals over the next fifteen years. His early friendships with the leading poets of mid-Victorian England ripened speedily. When he was in Ireland, he exchanged letters with his English friends, and his correspondence with Rossetti, Browning, and others is of great interest. In 1863, Allingham was appointed to the customs office in Lymington, Hampshire, and thereafter resided in England. Retiring from the civil service in 1870, he married in 1874. He acted as sub-editor of *Fraser's Magazine* under the editorship of James Anthony Froude and in 1874 succeeded Froude as editor.

Allingham's devotion to Ballyshannon, to Donegal, and to Ireland remained intense. At one moment in the 1860's, he was hoping for a pension that would enable him to devote the rest of his life entirely to a "deliberate study of Ireland, historical, topographical, and social."

Both Tennyson and Browning intervened with Gladstone, then Prime Minister, in support of the project, but it came to nothing. Allingham's love for Ireland was idiosyncratic. Politically he opposed Home Rule. Culturally, he opposed the revival of the Irish language. Yeats's opinion of his poetry, therefore, alternated between warm appreciation and a certain impatience.

In 1888, Yeats labelled him "the poet of Ballyshannon" and called him "non-national." "Non-national," repeated Allingham in his diary, and sardonically added, "how sad!" But in 1889 Yeats urged that Allingham be rediscovered. He regarded Allingham's poetry as technically competent and wished that other Irish poets had his "finish in the style," but complained that he was "the poet of Ballyshannon, though not of Ireland." However, Yeats said, if Allingham was "no national poet, he was at any rate, no thin-blooded cosmopolitan, but loved the hills around him and the land under his feet." For Yeats he was a "master of Irish song," along with de Vere, Ferguson, and Mangan. On balance it seems safe to say that despite Yeats's occasional strictures, he regarded Allingham as one of his favorites among the poets of the older generation. He included "Irish Poems"— presumably referring to *Irish Songs and Poems* (1887)— among the five best books of Irish verse on his two lists of the "Best Irish Books" drawn up in 1895.[2]

In Allingham's writings, then, there is much to interest the student of Irish literature. In *Laurence Bloomfield in Ireland* (1864; No. 61 in the Garland series), his novel in verse, he produced a significant work for the study of nineteenth-century Irish social history, an "authentic Irish classic," as Professor Malcolm Brown has recently called it. After running serially in *Fraser's Magazine* during 1862 and 1863, it was published as a book. When it first appeared, John O'Leary, the Fenian leader, a fanatical nationalist and cultivated student of literature, not only gave it high praise in the newly appearing Fenian newspaper, the *Irish People,* but also reprinted much of the text so that his subscribers would not have to buy the book. It was, as Brown says, "an impressive work and is impressive yet."[3] Yeats called it dull, despite its "stray felicities," and thought Allingham's shorter verse was better. Yet in Joyce's *Ulysses,* it stands on Bloom's bookshelves along with William O'Brien's novel, *When We Were Boys* (1890; No. 76).[4]

Written in rhymed iambic pentameter couplets reminiscent of George Crabbe's *Tales of the Hall* (1819), *Laurence Bloomfield* deals with the land problem. The hero, well-educated and well-traveled, at the age of twenty-six comes to reside on his Irish estates. The time is approximately 1855–1860, the scene, though not specified, surely Allingham's own Donegal. Bloomfield discovers that his agent, Pigot, has in his absence been behaving like all the villainous land agents we have encountered in Irish fiction since Maria Edgeworth's *Absentee* (1812; No. 4). Bloomfield's local fellow landowners are Orangemen, indifferent to the sufferings of the peasantry, which are described in moving detail.

Like Lord Colambre in *The Absentee* or "Mr. Easel" (who is really Lord Topertoe) in Carleton's *Valentine M'Clutchy* (1847; No. 40), Bloomfield investigates conditions,

> He visits Phelim's farm, and Pat's, and Mike's,
> And questions Pigot more than Pigot likes;

He has a program in mind:

> A kind just man would make the poor his
>   friends,
> And use his riches for no private ends;
> Till rich and poor, harmoniously conjoint,
> Form'd alto, basso, in a counterpoint.

But would this be possible in Ireland?

> But could he so in this distracted isle?
> Traditionary wrongs each heart defile,
> Received, inflicted, rankling, and renew'd;
> All passions shout the cries of ancient feud;
> God's worship is the pledge of endless hate:
> Who, linking class with class, these venoms can
>   abate?

He is unsure of himself and not anxious to overturn the existing situation, asking himself,

> Would things go better here, supposing I,
> Not Pigot, govern'd? ought I not to try?

The Catholic priest—who bans the ribbon oath—is treated with all respect and sympathy. Bloomfield idealistically wants the peasants to own their own farms, and faces the sneers of the local gentry. Of course, the ribbonmen are abroad in the land, and Pigot receives an anonymous warning. The young peasants are eager to join and do so even when their parents beg them not to;

> Neal fain would join that secret brotherhood,
> The rich men's terror; but his father shrewd,

> Who saw the 'Ninety-eight, and blamed alike
> The yeoman's pitch-cap, and the rebel's pike,
> Whose earliest memories were of houses
>   burning,
> Dead men from branches hung, and slowly
>   turning,
> Jack oft admonish'd him; and on her knees
> Maureen implored her son from thoughts like
>   these.
> Yet still he hanker'd for the fruit forbid:[5]

Allingham ranges himself with Carleton: he understands but disapproves of violence. Bloomfield realizes he must dismiss Pigot, and does so. Before the peasants have heard the news, however, the ribbonmen assassinate the agent.

But Bloomfield perseveres, and in the end Edgeworthian principles triumph. He gives lands rent-free until they are partly reclaimed, then asks for small rents, and finally—when the preliminary work is accomplished—gives fair leases. The strongest hands clear the brush and drain the bogs. The hovels and their dunghills give way to trim cottages and well-drained hillsides. Seven years transform the scene. Bloomfield's own mansion is weather-tight now; he collects and studies the ancient Irish relics to be found in the ground. He has promoted Neal, the erstwhile ribbonman, to be his steward. He has founded a school for both religions, which the clergy of both oppose, but which is a great success nonetheless. The tenantry are happy and loyal. Ribbonism has vanished and only the stubbornness of the local Orangemen and of the still recalcitrant landowners remains unconquered. Allingham has presented a moving vision of Bloomfield's dream fulfilled, all the more so as he has introduced us to the peasant families individually and made each the center of a human story. They are not mere symbols or factors in an economic equation, but human beings. The vision and its fulfillment had often been put forth previously by Irish writers but never with more pathos and persuasiveness.

Robert Lee Wolff

Notes

1. *The New Cambridge Bibliography of English Literature* III, 2nd
edition (Cambridge: University Press, 1969), has an entry on
Allingham, listing the writings about him down to the early
1960's, but omitting one article important for us: Patrick Mac-
Donough, "Laurence Bloomfield in Ireland," *The Dublin
Magazine* 25 (January-March, 1950), 25–33. *Anglo-Irish Litera-
ture. A Review of Research*, ed. R.J. Finneran (New York: Modern
Language Association of America, 1976), gives references to
useful studies published since 1969. Alan Warner, *William Al-
lingham* (Lewisburg: Bucknell University Press; and London:
Associated University Presses, 1975), the second of Warner's
books on Allingham, is a useful brief treatment, including a
chapter, pp. 43–57, on *Laurence Bloomfield.*

2. MacDonough, p. 33; Philip L. Marcus, *Yeats and the Beginning
of the Irish Renaissance* (Ithaca and London: Cornell University
Press, 1970), pp. 6, 15, 32, 97, 286.

3. Malcolm Brown, *The Politics of Irish Literature. From Thomas
Davis to William Butler Yeats* (Seattle: University of Washington
Press, 1972), p. 316.

4. MacDonough, p. 25; James Joyce, *Ulysses* (New York: Ran-
dom House, 1939), p. 693.

5. *Laurence Bloomfield,* pp. 13, 16, 59, 120–121.

LAURENCE BLOOMFIELD

IN IRELAND.

LAURENCE BLOOMFIELD

IN IRELAND.

A MODERN POEM.

By WILLIAM ALLINGHAM.

London and Cambridge:

MACMILLAN AND CO.

1864.

LONDON:
PRINTED BY R. CLAY, SON, AND TAYLOR,
BREAD STREET HILL.

CONTENTS.

———◆———

                                         PAGE

PREFACE vii

CHAPTER I.

LAURENCE 3

CHAPTER II.

NEIGHBOURING LANDLORDS 19

CHAPTER III.

A DINNER AT LISNAMOY HOUSE 37

CHAPTER IV.

THE DORANS 61

CHAPTER V.

BALLYTULLAGH 85

CHAPTER VI.

NEAL AT THE LOUGH 115

PAGE

CHAPTER VII.

TENANTS AT WILL 135

CHAPTER VIII.

A RIBBON LODGE 153

CHAPTER IX.

THE FAIR 177

CHAPTER X.

PIGOT 197

CHAPTER XI.

LORD AND LADY 221

CHAPTER XII.

MIDSUMMER 253

PREFACE.

IN this poem on every-day Irish affairs (a new and difficult, and for more than one reason a ticklish literary experiment), all readers who know Ireland will certainly see a good deal of truth, not taken up at second-hand; though on many points of opinion they are sure to differ from the writer, and from each other. It is free from personalities, and neither of an orange nor a green complexion; but it is Irish in phraseology, character, and local colour,—with as little use as might be of a corrupt dialect, and with no deference at all to the stage traditions of Paddyism. It first appeared in " Fraser's Magazine," and is now presented much revised and partly re-arranged.

The scene is a district in Ireland, of extent such as might be seen in panorama from a moderate eminence; inland, but not far from the coast, with mountain-range, hills, moors, and bogs, wide rich

plain, a river, and a lake. The persons are Sir
Ulick Harvey, an old landed proprietor; his nephew,
Mr. Bloomfield, a young one; Mr. Pigot, agent to
both; tenants upon each estate; with so much as
seemed proportionate respecting their wives, families,
and friends, neighbouring landlords, clergy, Ribbon-
men, politicians, &c. The parish is named Kilmoylan;
the hamlet, Ballytullagh, on Tullagh Hill; the town,
Lisnamoy; Sir Ulick's mansion, Lisnamoy House;
Mr. Bloomfield's, Croghan Hall, under Croghan
Mountain, and near Lough Braccan. In an Irish
whirlwind of contending interests and opinions,
Bloomfield finds his own way to a central spot of
peace in the heart of the storm.

Ireland, be it remembered, with two thousand miles
of coast-line, inclosing thirty-two counties, is not a
very small country, and is far from an homogeneous
one. To be *doctrinaire* on so large and complex a
subject is the furthest possible thing from the
present writer's intention.

March, 1864.

THE BOOK TO THE READER.

Good Sir, of whatsoever class or creed,
I am no wicked little Book indeed.
Preserve a kindly temper as you read.

We're one at heart, if you be Ireland's friend,
Though leagues asunder our opinions tend.
There are but two great parties in the end.

LAURENCE BLOOMFIELD IN IRELAND.

CHAPTER I.

LAURENCE BLOOMFIELD
IN IRELAND.

A MODERN POEM,

IN TWELVE CHAPTERS.

I.

LAURENCE.

AUTUMNAL sunshine spread on Irish hills   1

Imagination's bright'ning mirror fills,

Wherein a Horseman on a handsome grey

Along the high road takes his easy way,

Saluted low by every ragged hat,   5

Saluting kindly every Teague and Pat

Who plods the mud or jolts on lazy wheels,

Or loudly drives a patient ass with creels,[1]

---

[1] *creels,* panniers.

(Short pipe removed before obeisance made)
Or checks, regardant, his potato-spade ;   10
" Fine day," the young man says with friendly nod,
" Fine day, your honour,—glory be to God !"
Then, too polite to stare, they talk their fill
Of Minor Bloomfield (so they call him still,
Though six-and-twenty now) come back of late   15
From foreign countries to his own estate,
And who in turn has no incurious eye
For each, and all the world, in passing by ;
The cornstacks seen through rusty sycamores,
Pigs, tatter'd children, pools at cabin doors,   20
Unshelter'd rocky hill-sides, browsed by sheep,
Summer's last flow'rs that nigh some brooklet creep,
Black flats of bog, stone-fences loose and rough,
A thorn-branch in a gap thought gate enough,
And all the wide and groveless landscape round,   25
Moor, stubble, aftermath, or new-plough'd ground,
Where with the crows white seagulls come to pick ;
Or many a wasteful acre crowded thick

With docken, coltsfoot, and the hoary weed
Call'd fairy-horse, and tufted thistle-seed   30
Which *for* the farm, *against* the farmer tells ;
Or wrinkled hawthorns shading homestead wells,
Or, saddest sight, some ruin'd cottage-wall,
The roof-tree cut, the rafters forced to fall
From gables with domestic smoke embrown'd,   35
Where Poverty at worst a shelter found,
The scene, perhaps, of all its little life,
Its humble joys, and unsuccessful strife.
Th' observant rider pass'd too many such ;
Let them do more (he thought) who do so much,   40
Nor, where they've kill'd a human dwelling-place,
Unburied leave the skeleton's disgrace.
Though Irish, he was of the absentees,
And unaccustom'd yet to sights like these.

    At twelve years old his birthplace he had left, 45
A child endow'd with much, of much bereft ;
Return'd a boy—a lad—the third time now

Returns, a man, with broad and serious brow.
A younger son (the better lot at first),
And by a Celtic peasant fondly nurst,   50
Bloomfield is Irish born and English bred,
Surviving heir of both his parents dead ;
One who has studied, travell'd, lived, and thought,
Is brave, and modest, as a young man ought ;
Calm—sympathetic ; hasty—full of tact ;   55
Poetic, but insisting much on fact ;
A complex character and various mind,
Where all, like some rich landscape, lies combined.

From school to Ireland, Laurence first return'd
A patriot vow'd ; his soul for Ireland burn'd.   60
Oft did his schoolmates' taunts in combat end,
And high his plans with one Hibernian friend,
Who long'd like him for manhood, to set free
Their emerald Inisfail from sea to sea,
With army, senate, all a nation's life,   65
Copartner in the great world's glorious strife,

Peer in all arts, gay rival in each race,

Illustrious, firm, in her peculiar place.

The glories and the griefs of Erin fill'd

Heart and imagination. How he thrill'd   70

To every harp-note of her aneient fame,

How, to her storied wounds, his cheek would flame !

And hearing some great speaker, on a day,

Whose urgent grasp held thousands under sway

While thus he thunder'd,—" 'Tis for slaves alone 75

" To live without a country of their own !

" Alas for Ireland ! she whose sons are born

" The wide earth's pity and proud England's scorn,

" England whose fraud and guilt have sunk us low.

" Speak, Irishmen, shall this be always so ?"   80

Judge how young Laurence felt. " Like a young fool,"

His guardian growl'd, and shipp'd him back to school.

   Not such was he at Cambridge ; for he found

Thought's new horizons daily opening round,

While History spread her pictures grave and vast ; 85

And living Britain startled him at last
To recognise the large imperial tone,
And all the grandeur of a well-built throne.
O joy, a part in England's pride to claim,
To flush with triumph in her force and fame,   90
See distant powers confess with wondering awe
Her martial strength, her majesty of law,
And every child of hers throughout the world
Stand safe beneath her banner, broad unfurl'd !

A beardless Burke of college parliament   95
The loyal Laurence back to Ireland went,
On visit to a rich relation's house ;
Where boldly to Sir Ulick he avows
An alter'd mind, and sees with alter'd sight
Reckless provincials, hating rule and right,   100
Busy for mischief without aim or sense,
Their politics mere factious turbulence,
Drawn this and that way by the word or nod
Of noisy rogues and stealthy men-of-God ;

And checks them with a small ideal band   105
Who, brothers, round the British Ensign stand,
To face rebellion, Papistry, and crime,
With staunchness proved in many a perilous time.
At twenty-one, his too a place shall hold
With names ancestral in the Lodge enroll'd ;   110
Or thus at least resolved the young man, eager-soul'd.

I then knew Laurence first, and could descry
Keen intellect and generous sympathy
In every look ; life's fountain fresh and bright
In him, for one man, freely sprang to light.   115
Full was his nostril, sensitive his mouth,
His candid brow capacious of the truth ;
Eyes, good Hibernian, warmest of all greys,
Fervent and clear, or veil'd in thoughtful haze ;
Locks loosely curling, 'twixt a black and brown ; 120
His lips and chin, though but in boyhood's down,
Were sculptured boldly, to confirm the face ;
A slender figure swayed with careless grace

To every impulse, every varying mood;

Nothing in him was formal, nothing rude.   125

The first five minutes rank'd him as a friend,

He still was new and rare at five years' end.

  Gowns, books, degrees, will leave a fool a fool,

But wit is best when wit has gone to school.

In busy leisure 'mid those cloisters grey,   130

This young man communed many a happy day

With thoughts perennial of the mighty dead,

To which his soul, how often, whilst he redd,

Sprang up with greeting; nor, in prose or rhyme,

Fail'd he to mark the Spirit of the Time;   135

Then wander'd forth, saw Germany and Greece,

France, fairer Italy, with large increase

For that eternal storehouse in the mind;

Saw, too, earth's younger half, whose western wind

Would bear across the sea, if wind could bear,   140

To Ireland many a wish and filial pray'r.

And now he treads again the shamrock shore,

Of age, and half a fruitful decade more ;
By books, by travel, and by life matured,
With words less ready, insight more assured,   145
A student still, of all beneath the sun,
And wishing good to each, and wrong to none.

  His life, the first great impulse falling slack,
Has now begun to feel or fear a lack,
Unknown, undreamt-of hitherto, a void,   15
A need in truth for work ; to rise employ'd
Each morning-light on some progressive toil,
Itself not all inadequate, the foil
And clasp for ruby, pearl, and diamond hours,
Or say, the root and stem for life's best flow'rs. 155
Public ambitions are not to his mind,
His nature's proper work seems hard to find,
Grown sick of London's huge and flimsy maze,
Polite, luxurious, ineffectual days.
But no such turn suspect his English friends ;   160
This morning, Frederick Stanley's letter ends-

' Your Blessed Island I have also seen,
'At Galway Claddagh, Dublin Castle, been,
'And view'd the savage natives, high and low

~~'And view'd savages that is, high and low,~~

' Not unamusing for a month or so ;   165
'But fancy living in the place !—take care
' And don't get shot, old fellow, whilst you're there.'
So Stanley. Meanwhile, fain are other some
To keep the youth in Ireland, now he's come.

Greatly his friends and relatives desire   170
To colour staring blue the rich young Squire,
With vivid streaks of orange, to describe
A noble chieftain of their loyal tribe,
That in such war-paint he may lead their van
To fight the county with a fierce Green Man.   175
But soon they find this Bloomfield less and more
Than lived in their philosophy before ;
Direct and frank in motive, plan, and deed,
Cautious and mild in theory and creed,
There friendly, here reserved, but not by rule,   180

Like those who send their cordial smile to school;
Cold upon interests where the rest grow hot,
Intent, where they have never given a thought;
Too apt to lightly leap 'the usual course,'
Turn, look about,—he may perhaps do worse ;   185
He visits Phelim's farm, and Pat's, and Mike's,
And questions Pigot more than Pigot likes ;
Each tenant's history fain would understand,
Examines every corner of his land,
Day after day has freely seen and heard,   190
But of his general thought avows no word ;
Perhaps, in secret, striving to arrange
Experiences so multiform and strange.

Thus much of Laurence Bloomfield, on his way
From Croghan Hall, this bright autumnal day,   195
Quickly, by turns, and slowly, man and beast,
To where Sir Ulick Harvey spreads the feast,
Twice, a well-arm'd police patrol he met,
To guard the dinner-party duly set.

Beyond the dirty town an Irish mile,   200

Thick laurels round Sir Ulick's gateway smile ;

A mail'd arm cut on either pillar-stone

Defends the Harvey motto, doubly shown,

Meis, ut placet, utens ; gravel-spread,

And dusk with boughs that whisper overhead,   205

A private drive at every turn displays

The vista'd park where silky cattle graze,

Through clumps of flow'rs and greensward sweeping
        wide

Unfolds the heavy mansion's front of pride,

And whirls, if such felicity be yours,   210

Your chariot to the gently awful doors,

Where men of soft address and portly frame,

With gorgeous garments, wait to breathe your name.

Lisnamoy House can see far summits rise

In azure bloom, or cold on misty skies,   215

Above the broad plantation set to screen

Those dismal wastes of bog that stretch between ;

The Village, northward, only shows a spire,

As humbly conscious of the haughty Squire,
Whose Lady visits but the Vicar's wife,   220
Each meaner building crouchant for its life ;
And groves yet thick, though change is on the
          trees,

Their first light losses borne on every breeze,
Shut out from view a thousand vulgar fields,
Whose foison great Sir Ulick's grandeur yields,   225
With many a roof of thatch, where daily toil
Extorts the bread of man from earth's dull soil.

'This must be : and if Toil receive his share,
'Nor Gather'd Power be selfish and unfair,
'Toil will not grudge Inheritance or Gain,   230
'The part which these in manly mood sustain.
'Toil, Poverty, are tolerable things,—
'Injustice every human spirit wrings;
'*Thence* flows the bitter stream of discontent,
'For him that earns a wage or pays a rent,   235

' As through the patriot's pulses, born to feel

' His country's wounds, and glow with angry zeal.'

Thus meditated Bloomfield, while his horse

Turn'd to familiar stableyard his course.

' A   kind   just   man   would   make   the   poor   his
                friends,   240

' And use his riches for no private ends ;

' Till rich and poor, harmoniously conjoint,

' Form'd alto, basso, in a counterpoint.

' But could he so in this distracted isle ?

' Traditionary wrongs each heart defile,   245

' Received, inflicted, rankling, and renew'd ;

' All passions shout the cries of ancient feud ;

' God's worship is the pledge of endless hate :

' Who, linking class with class, these venoms can
                abate ?

' How, once I quit the glorious world of dreams,   250

' Begin, where all a vile confusion seems ?

' Perchance these Irish Captains, view'd aright,

' Sustain as best they may an ugly fight.

'So let them. I'll interrogate the Sphinx,

'And Him who sleeps at Philæ, for the links   255

'Of past and future; and behold the while

'Great dawns and sunsets mirror'd in the Nile.'

LAURENCE BLOOMFIELD IN IRELAND.

CHAPTER II.

NEIGHBOURING LANDLORDS.

LAURENCE BLOOMFIELD

IN IRELAND.

II.

NEIGHBOURING LANDLORDS.

THIS Irish county bears an evil name,   1
And Bloomfield's district stands the worst in fame,
For agitation, discord, threats, waylayings,
Fears and suspicions, plottings and betrayings ;
Beasts kill'd and maim'd, infernal fires at night,   5
Red murder stalking free in full daylight.
That landlords and their tenants lived as foes
He knew, as one a truth by hearsay knows,
But now it stands around where'er he goes.

    Blue mountains, dusky moorlands, verdant   10
        plain ;

A lively river hastening to the main ;
Bog, arable, and pasture ; lake and pond,
And woody park ; a little Town beyond ;
Wide-scatter'd human dwellings, great and small ;
Glance round one rural scene ; and let me call　15
Its roll of petty princes,—they are such,
If ruling little of our world, or much.
Laws and a suzerain above them stand,
But have they not dominion in the land ?

　The realm of Bloomfield, late his uncle's ward, 20
And that which owns Sir Ulick for its lord,
Pigot now governs, agent wise and great,
Rich man himself, grand juror, magistrate.
'Twas taught as part of Bloomfield's early creed,
' Pigot—in-val-uable man indeed !'　　　　　25
And though Sir Ulick loves to seem to reign,
Pigot's least whisper never falls in vain.
You find in old Sir Ulick Harvey's face,
The looks of long command, and comely race ;

No small man sees a brother in those eyes   30
Of calm and frosty blue, like winter skies ;
Courteous his voice, yet all the pride is there,
Pride like a halo crowns his silvery hair ;
'Tis unmisgiving pride that makes him frank
With humble folk, and dress beneath his rank.   35
Born in the purple, he could hardly know
Less of the tides of life that round him flow.
The Laws were for the Higher Classes made ;
But while the Lower gratefully obey'd,
To patronize them you had his consent,   40
Promote their comfort, to a safe extent,
And teach them—just enough, and not too much ;
Most careful lest with impious hand you touch
Order and grade as plann'd by Providence.
An apothegm, no doubt, of weighty sense ;   45
Had he but ask'd, is prejudice of mine
A perfect measure of the Will Divine ?
Or, by how much per annum is one given
A seat as privy-councillor of Heaven ?

He sometimes took a well-meant scheme in   50
    hand,
Which must be done exactly as he plann'd ;
His judgment feeble, and his self-will strong,
He had his way, and that was mostly wrong.
The whim was such, that seized his mind of late,
To ' square ' the farms on all his wide estate ;   55
Tim's mountain grazing, Peter's lough-side patch,
This onion-field of Ned's that few could match,
Phil's earliest ridges, Thady's bog, worse hap !
By mere new lines across his Honour's map
From ancient holdings have been clipt away,   60
Despite the loud complaints, or dumb dismay.

  My Lady Harvey comes of Shropshire blood,
Stately, with finish'd manners, cold of mood ,
Her eldest son is in the Guards ; her next
At Eton ; her two daughters—I'm perplex'd   65
To specify young ladies—they are tall,
Dark-hair'd, and smile in speaking, that is all.

Joining Sir Ulick's at the river's bend,
Lord Crasher's acres east and west extend ;
Great owner here, in England greater still.   70
As poor folk say, 'The world's divided ill.'
On every pleasure men can buy with gold
He surfeited ; and now, diseased and old,
He lives abroad ; a firm in Molesworth Street
Doing what their attorneyship thinks meet.   75
The rule of *seventy* properties have they.
Wide waves the meadow on a summer day,
Far spread the sheep across the swelling hill,
And horns and hooves the daisied pasture fill ;
A stout and high enclosure girdles all,   80
Built up with stones from many a cottage wall ;
And, thanks to Phinn & Wedgely's thrifty
          pains,
Not one unsightly ruin there remains.
Phinn comes half-yearly, sometimes with a friend,
Who writes to *Mail* or *Warder* to commend   85
These vast improvements, and bestows the term

Of 'Ireland's benefactors' on the firm,
A well-earn'd title, in the firm's own mind.
Twice only in the memory of mankind
Lord Crasher's proud and noble self appear'd ;   90
Up-river, last time, in his yacht he steer'd,
With crew of seven, a valet, a French cook,
And one on whom askance the gentry look,
Although a pretty, well-dress'd demoiselle,—
Not Lady Crasher, who, as gossips tell,   95
Goes her own wicked way. They stopp'd a
        week ;

Then, with gay ribbons fluttering from the peak,
And snowy skirts spread wide, on either hand
The *Aphrodite* curtsied to the land,
And glided off. My Lord, with gouty legs,   100
Drinks Baden-Baden water, and life's dregs,
With cynic jest inlays his black despair,
And curses all things from his easy chair.
Yearly, the Honourable George, his son,
To Ireland brings his game-subduing gun ;   105

Who labours hard and hopes he shall succeed
To make the pheasant in those copses breed.

Finlay, next landlord (I'll abridge the tale),
Prince of Glenawn, a low and fertile vale,
No fool by birth, but hard, and praised for   110
        wise
The more he learn'd all softness to despise,
Married a shrew for money, louts begot,
Debased his wishes to a vulgar lot,
To pence and pounds coin'd all his mother-wit,
And ossified his nature bit by bit.   115
A dull cold home, devoid of every grace,
Distrust and dread in each dependent's face,
Bullocks and turnips, mighty stacks of grain,
Plethoric purse, impoverish'd heart and brain,—
Such Finlay's life; and when that life shall end,   120
He'll die as no man's debtor, no man's friend.
Who duns?—who loves him? he can pay his way;
' A hard but honest man,' as people say.

Unlike this careful management (between
The two, Sir Ulick's townlands intervene)   125
Is that of Termon on the river-side,
Domain and mansion of insolvent pride,
Where Dysart, drawing from ancestral ground
One sterling penny for each phantom pound
Of rent-roll, lives, when all the truth is known, 130
Mere factor in the place he calls his own ;
Through mortgages and bonds, one wide-spread maze,
Steps, dances, doubles round by devious ways,
While creditor, to creditor a foe,
Hangs dubious o'er the vast imbroglio.   135
And thus, minute in bargain where he can,
There, closing quick with ready-money man,
Despised for cunning, and for malice fear'd,
Yet still by custom and old name endear'd
To Celtic minds, who also better like   140
A rule of thumb than Gough's arithmetic,—
Dysart has shuffled on, to this good day,
Let creditors and courts do what they may.

The house is wondrous large, and wondrous mean;
Its likeness year by year more rarely seen;   145
A ragged billiard-table decks the hall,
Abandon'd long ago of cue and ball,
With whips and tools and garments litter'd o'er,
And lurking dogs possess the dangerous floor.
Ghost, from Proconsul Rutland's time, show in   150
To this great shabby room, which heard the din
Of bet and handicap, oath, toast, and song,
From squires and younger sons, a vanish'd throng,
Who drank much wine, who many foxes slew,
Hunted themselves by creditors all through,   155
And caught at last, or fairly run to earth;
A cold and ghastly room of bygone mirth.
Above the dusty fox's-brush see hung
Our grandpapa the Major, spruce and young,
In faded scarlet; on that other side   160
The needy Viscount's daughter, his fair bride;
And many portraits with once-famous names,
Of ancestors and horses, dogs and dames,

Now damp, or smutch'd, or dropping from their frames.

Big doleful house it is, with many a leak;   165

With dingy passages and bedrooms bleak;

With broken window-panes and mildew'd walls;

With grass-grown courtyard and deserted stalls

That proudly echoed to the hunting-stud,

Where still one stable shows its 'bit of blood.'   170

Tom is not wed; long wed is brother Hugh;

They seldom meet, and quarrel when they do.

Tom is a staunch good Protestant by creed,

But half a Mormon, judged by act and deed;

A dozen wives he has, but underhand,   175

Sub rosâ, not confess'd, you understand,

And this makes all the difference, of course.

His pretty little babes, except perforce,

He never knows, and never wants to know;

Yet, clippings of his purse must that way go.   180

Pass on to Isaac Brown, a man elect,

Wesleyan stout, our wealthiest of his sect;

Who bought and still buys land, none quite sees
     how,

Whilst all his shrewdness and success allow.

On Crasher's mortgage he has money lent,   185

He takes a quiet bill at ten per cent.,

The local public business much he sways,

He's learn'd in every neighbour's means and ways,

For comfort cares, for fashion not a whit,

Nor if the gentry to their ranks admit.   190

All preachers love him ; he can best afford

The unctuous converse and the unctuous board ;

Ev'n the poor nag, slow-rattling up the road

In ancient rusty gig a pious load,

Wags his weak tail, and strikes a brisker trot,   195

Approaching Brownstown, Isaac's pleasant lot.

For though at Poor-House Board was never known

A flintier Guardian-angel than good Brown,

As each old hag and shivering child can tell,—

Go dine with Isaac, and he feeds you well.   200

And hear him pray, with fiercely close-shut eyes!
Gentle at first the measured accents rise,
But soon he waxes loud, and storms the skies.
Deep is the chest, and powerful bass the voice,
The language of a true celestial choice ;   205
Handorgan-wise the holy phrases ground,
Go turning and returning round and round ;
The sing-song duly runs from low to high ;
The choruss'd groans at intervals reply ;
Till after forty minutes' sweat and din,   210
Leaving perhaps too little prayer within,
Dear Brother Brown, athletic babe of grace,
Resumes his bench, and wipes his reeking face.
And if among his audience may be found
One who received two shillings in the pound   215
When merchant Isaac, twenty years ago,—
Then talking pious too, but meek and low,
Was chasten'd by the Lord,—with what delight
Must he behold the comfortable plight
And sacred influence of this worthy man.   220

Isaac can put in awe, he only can,
The very preachers ; oily though his lip,
His will and temper have a stubborn grip.
His son, a scamp, and always in disgrace,
Skulks from the father's unforgiving face.   225
His timid, sickly wife is sore afraid.
His three stout daughters dare not go array'd
Too smartly, but read novels unconfess'd.
Brown, of all neighbouring owners handles best
Conacre and subletting ; he can boast   230
That poorest tenants profit him the most.

One other Landlord, to conclude our list :
O'Hara,—*The* O'Hara, some insist,—
Of princely Irish race, which sounds full well ;
But what an Irish prince was, who can tell ?   235
It more imports to study wisely how
They rule the world who stand for Princes now.
The present Chief, a thin-faced man of care,
Keeps here his Bailiff, but resides elsewhere ;

A widower he, some fifty-two years old,   240
A rigid Catholic, mild, formal, cold.
Children he had, but death removed his sons,
He lock'd his youthful daughters up as nuns ;
An heir for half his wealth he may select ;
His Clergy use him with profound respect.   245
O'Hara, once ambitious, all in vain,
And indisposed for action or for gain,
Disgusted long since with a public life,
Hates England's name, but censures noisy strife ;
Is proud, dyspeptic, taciturn, and shy,   250
Learn'd in forgotten trifles, dead and dry ;
Secluded from the troublous world he lives,
And secret help to church and convent gives.
Low-let, ill-till'd, and unimproved, his lands
Are left in lazy, sneaking flatterers' hands,   255
Most of them of his Bailiff-steward's tribe,
Nor any who withhold that rascal's bribe.

    Lord Crasher, The O'Hara, Isaac Brown,

Sir Ulick, Dysart, Finlay,—here set down
With touch of rapid pencil, not untrue,   260
Are one horizon's dominating few,
With Pigot's name to add, and Bloomfield's own :
Eight Lords of Land, terrestrial gods, are shown.

Some part of whom, with others not so great,
Consulting on the country's dreadful state,   265
Sir Ulick Harvey towering in the chair,
Impressively, resolved, that then and there
They sat assembled : that resolved they were
That something should be done : and what to do—
But this was more than they exactly knew.   270
From first to last 'twas cordially agreed
That tenants had been kindly used indeed
By every landlord round.   Who justly blamed ?
With modest boldness for themselves they claim'd
Approval of the world : their simple rights.   275
Were never half enforced.

                              Warm days and nights

Fulfill'd the harvest to the reaper's hook;
But souls of men dismay and passion shook.
It should have been a peaceful, grateful time;   280
But o'er this landscape enmity and crime
Like shadow lay. The harvesting is done;
That shadow stays, in spite of moon or sun.

LAURENCE BLOOMFIELD IN IRELAND.

CHAPTER III.

A DINNER AT LISNAMOY HOUSE.

LAURENCE BLOOMFIELD

IN IRELAND.

III.

A DINNER AT LISNAMOY HOUSE.

CHILLY and dim th' autumnal fields; but bright   1
Sir Ulick's table glows with waxen light;
Alternate fair and brown, the seemly guests
With smiling nonsense aid the varied zests;
The solemn liveries with observance wait,   5
And smoothly pour the wine and shift the plate;
Each thing fulfils a justly measured part,
And all like nature seems, where all is art.
The steps of banquet keeping time and place,
With bland succession and unconscious grace,   10
The dishes circle in a savoury train,
The small-talk bubbles with the brisk champagne;

Till Beauty now glides rustling from the room,
And men in freer groups their chairs resume.

  Say who they are, whom Irish Fates combine 15
To crack those filberts and to sip that wine ?
The pompous Head of all the Harvey clan ;
Shrewd Vicar Boyd, who seems a simple man ;
Lord Crasher's son, with whiskers large and fair,
His chief distinction, and his fondest care ;   20
Hard Finlay ; Laurence Bloomfield next in place ;
Fat Agent Pigot with his joking face ;
James Duff, a northern tory, big and coarse ;
Dysart, who shrewdly bets on dog and horse ;
With these, great Nassau Blunderbore, whose fame 25
Fills all the journals,—hear him now declaim,
When Bloomfield, sifting out some little fact,
Would fain have answer quiet and exact :
" All Papists are but rebels in disguise,
" And if they dared, this very night would rise ; 30
" The law from mere compulsion they obey,

" Their priests and demagogues have genuine sway ;

" Mainly the first, a dark and dangerous band,

" The creeping rulers of this wretched land,

" Their faith a lie, their purity a cheat,   35

" (Want of detection proves their plans complete)

" Dogmatic vassals of insidious Rome,

" Courted by coward governments at home,

" Ambitious, cunning, false, yet firm of will,—

" Improve them, you but help their power of ill. 40

" Each Papist is his Queen's and Landlord's foe,

" And every Priest conspires to keep him so !"

Such is the well-worn theme.   Such theme to-
          night

Great Nassau pounds with fourfold main and might ;

For Ribbonism has flourish'd high its head,—   45

Has sworn a trembling farmer, dragg'd from bed,

To quash his lawsuit,—promised mortal harm

To him who ventures on the vacant farm

Snatch'd from a poor industrious innocent,

Whose only fault was owing five years' rent,—   50

Puts fear and hate, acknowledged or conceal'd,

To haunt each hearth, and lurk in every field.

Boyd listens blandly, Boyd the shrewd divine,

Who loves his money, and who likes his wine,

Who travels, has a house in Mountjoy-square,   55

And to his parish comes for change of air,

Blames, ex-officio, popery and dissent,

Though doctrines breed him little discontent,

Lets parish questions to the Curate go,

(The Curate's views   are 'high,' his pay but

          low)—   60

A trim old parson, Boyd ; whose smile urbane

Will soothe, although perhaps you talk in vain ;

Blest with four daughters, and, as fame resounds,

For each a fortune of five thousand pounds.

The first is clever—writeth books, be sure ;   65

The second Sunday-schools the drowsy poor

By rote, on unintelligible things ;

Another of the damsels plays and sings ;

The fourth professes, merely, flaxen curls.

What is their mother?—slave to these four girls. 70

  " I can't think ill of every popish priest,"

Says Boyd,—" our own are harmless men, at least;

" Vulgar no doubt, and very wrong, of course,

" But still, admit the truth, we might have worse."

  " Sir!" responds   Nassau, (Bloomfield   in   his

           eye)   75

" We live amidst one huge conspiracy!

" For Papal Ireland hates, in common cause,

" The church, the constitution, and the laws.

" Priest, politicians, with their cunning views,

" The blindfold passions of the peasants use;   80

" This wicked league if once their Altar spoke

" Would break and vanish, like a ring of smoke.

" Some feign rebuke,—the clients comprehend,

"And feel them twitch the blood-stain'd Ribbon's

           end."

"Why !" angry Duff breaks in, "to crown it all, 85

"Here's Pigot threaten'd in a murder-scrawl.

"Sooner than let this Ballytullagh stand,

"I'd tear it down, by Jove, with my own hand,—

"For in such times as these, we, by the Lord !

"Must do our duty, and with one accord.   90

"Elections too draw near, and if we flinch

"They'll seize an ell—a mile—for every inch.

"By George I leave no man of mine in doubt,—

"Vote as I bid you, or I turn you out!"

True Orangemen were Blunderbore and Duff,   95

Each spoke his mind, and each made noise enough ;

The one on force of argument relied,

The argument of force was all the other's pride.

"These people, on the side of Tullagh Hill,"

Says Agent Pigot, "merely hold at will   100

"Some spots of tillage in a mountain tract,

"O'er which they stray'd, and deem'd it theirs in fact.

"Half-savage long, reduced to bounds at last,

" From grumbling to defiance they have pass'd ;

" With men and money help the Ribbon Lodge; 105

" Full time, I think, to ask our friends to budge !

" To get his own, Sir Ulick would have paid,

" But this have I, on principle, gainsaid ;

" These folk deserve no kindness, have no claim ;

" Count down fee-simple, they would yell the same.

" Faith, gentlemen, this country sorely needs   111

" A quicker clearance of its human weeds ;

" But still, the proper system is begun,

" And forty holdings we shall change to one."

Bloomfield, his inexperience much confess'd,   115

Doubts if the large dispeopled farms be best,—

Best in a wide sense, best for all the world,

(At this expression sundry lips were curl'd)—

" I wish, but know not how, each peasant's hand

" Might work, nay, hope to win, a share of land ; 120

" For ownership, however small it be,

" Breeds diligence, content, and loyalty,

" And tirelessly compels the rudest field,

"Inch after inch, its very most to yield.

" Wealth might its true prerogatives retain ;   125

" And no man lose, and all men greatly gain."

This, Bloomfield chiefly to the Vicar said,

Who courteously demurr'd with shake of head.

" Ah, my dear sir, our philanthropic dreams

" Are fine—but human nature mars our schemes ! " 130

If Boyd had such, he well knew how to shake

Those dreams away, and thus live wide-awake.

Loud hemm'd Sir Ulick, in his pompous tone,

A platitudinarian too-well known,

Whom meetings with respectful torpor heard,   135

And all his private circle duly fear'd.

How polish'd, grave, and dignified he is,

Strutting along in dull periphrasis,

With mental back impossible to bend !

Pinchbeck he quotes, his economic friend,   140

That 'tenant-right' is robbery or worse ;

That 'little holdings' are a country's curse ;
Does he that merely tills turn owner ?   Why,
Who could inherit land, who sell or buy ?—
Which may have reason in it : but at best   145
Pinchbeck in some poor scrap of truth is drest,
And, like the Kaffir who has chanced to find
A coat of Europe, dons it front-behind.

Now Finlay, of the cold sarcastic eye,
And voice for ever tuneless, hard, and dry :   150
" Land is of course, like other things you buy,
" Investment for your money.   Find or make
" A contract,—law will punish if you break.
"Supposing legal contract there be none,
" Then, he who occupies your house in town,   155
" Or country farm (what matters which) must know
" That when the owner. bids him, he should go.
·' He has no lease, though he desires to stay,
" Why, then, so much the worse for him, you say.
" He has a lease, and pays but little rent,   160

" A lucky man ! and you must bide content ;

" He wants a lease ; then, such and such the terms,

" Or you declare you will not let your farms.

" Contracts are contracts ; law is law ; and land

" Is property : thus much I understand.'   165

    Fat Pigot turn'd to every one who spoke,

And laugh'd when each was done, as at a joke.

His fun is somewhat threadbare, but you half

Believe it rich, so hearty is his laugh ;

And not ill-furnish'd he with jest and tale.   170

Beetroot beside his glowing cheek were pale.

Kind to his household, jolly with his friends,

Business begun, all Pigot's feeling ends ;

With jovial voice and look, his hand, like Fate's

Can freeze the dwellers upon four estates,   175

Whose slavish flattery finds a self-redress,

A sort of freedom, in its own excess.

Their mother-wit,—debased through dismal years

Of rapine and oppression, blood and tears,

To craft and cunning,—twists in reptile form,   180
A slimy, soft, and poison-bearing worm.
Be silent, noisy tongues on either shore!
Denounce, defend, recriminate no more!
In history's record England reads her blame,
Ireland her grief, her folly, and her shame;   185
Let each peruse with humble soul and sage,
And, from the past, amend the future page.

But, meanwhile, of the Present shall be redd
One dirty leaf,—a coffin decks its head,—
From Pigot's bulky pocket, by desire,   190
Emitted, for the table to admire:
'Take Notis, Big gut, if one claw you lay
'On Tullah, you'll for ever roo the day—
'So change your tune, and quickly, or by God
'This warnin is your last—we'll have your blud. 195
'Sined, Captin Starlite.'

                    —"Funny letter, eh?"

The Honourable George is heard to say.

E

" Good mark "—says Dysart, with a nod and laugh.

" For pot-shots," Duff observes, " too good by half."

"Got a six-shooter ?" Tom rejoins : "let's see." 200

" No !" cry the rest. Says Pigot, " Trust to me,"

And hides the weapon. Tom approves not such :

" I'll bet, with your revolver, you don't touch

" My hat at twenty yards, two shots in five.

"You must have daily practice, man alive !   205

" Practice is everything, and firing quick,

" Before a lazy finger does the trick ;

" That's how my uncle finish'd Major Crowe,

" A splendid marksman, only rather slow.

" Fire from the hip !" cries Tom in cheerful mood, 210

And cracks a nut in proper attitude.

—" Mayn't get the chance," growls Finlay.

                                        It was time,

Sir Ulick thought, to meet this growth of crime,

But how ?—shall counter-terror bid it cease

By Proclamation and more big Police ?   215

Spies and rewards, thought Dysart ; turning out

All tenants, Duff said, in one rabble-rout.
" Where should they go to?" " They may go to h—."
But Bloomfield to his own reflections fell :
' Owners are owners we decide in haste,—   220
' Might three men choose to keep a county waste ?
' Is there no spirit in the world of things
' Whereon his gyve in vain the lawyer flings ?
' Can we, by politics of coin or birth,
' Own, like a house or hunter, God's round earth? 225
' Or, is that different property ? We're tried
' In turn as leaders. Families subside,
' As they have risen, like billows of a tide,—
' Heirs lifted to the top-surge one by one.
' But continuity from sire to son,   230
' No further, quibbles in the North-star's face :
' One man is dead—another's in his place.
' A trust, to help our fellow-men, we own ;
' True right of property is this alone.
' Chieftains there must be ; and the low man
        clings   235

' With long affection to unworthy kings ;
' Ev'n here, would fain be faithful to his lord '—
And Bloomfield sigh'd and look'd around the board.
' To throw my life to loss with men like these ?—
' Why   should   I ?'—of   a   sudden   this   brought
   ease.   240

' Where earth gives most of what to me is best
' To live is mine, my privilege confess'd,
' My duty too '—but here some side-wind caught
The sail out-spread of his quick-moving thought :
Duty with duty it is hard to weigh,   245
To rule the very power you must obey,
Doubt Judgment, of your doubting doubtful too.
The pain of too much freedom Bloomfield knew.
For all the choice was in his proper hand ;
No shadow-barrier in his road to stand   250
Of others' expectation ; none could say,
Parting next week, that he had plann'd to stay,
Nor wonder if th' ensuing seven years' rent
In banker's bills should over sea be sent,

While Pigot, well-accustom'd viceroy, reign'd,   255
And far off tenants fruitlessly complain'd.
While Bloomfield's mind experienced this unrest,
His face was calm, his converse self-possest ;
The noble sprig beside him sees no gloom ;
"Come down to shoot the country, I presume ?   260
"Good cocking in Sir Ulick's upper wood—
"Cover for grouse on Croghan, doocid good.
"Queer fellows, though, the common fellows round—·
"And every one a poacher—does your ground
"Touch on the river?"

                   So we sit and talk,   265
A finger round the crystal flower-bell-stalk
Brimm'd with   cool   claret,   fruit   and   biscuits
       munch,
And some in secret pine for whisky-punch,
Or vapour of the soothing weed. But soon
All reassemble in the White Saloon,   270
With decent forms of speech and gestures fit,
Which clothe mere dulness with a kind of wit.

   Though press'd to stay, and bid with serious brow

Remember he is not in England now,

Laurence will homeward ride, and ride alone ;   275

Deaf, blind, insensible as stock or stone

To three Miss Harveys and to four Miss Boyds,

The charm of song and every smile avoids,

Yielding that bower of beauty and of tea

To George's whiskers, and our mild A.B.,   280

Too busy Curate to present more soon

His well-brush'd hair and voice's gentle croon.

How does a man with seventy pounds a-year

In virgin linen every day appear ?

Spotless his shirts are, spotless too his life ;   285

Stiff in cravat, and dialectic strife,

He shuns the popish priests, and flogs the Pope,

Nor may the Methodist for mercy hope ;

Much milk of human kindness, too, he carries,

A little sour'd with dogma, through the parish,   290

And plays a half-divine, half-human part

With many a pious flirting female heart.

Enough—on dangerous matter we presume ;

Shut smoothly, door of silken drawing-room !

Let Lady Harvey lead the reverend man   295

Profoundly to discuss his favourite plan

Whereby we might convert all Papists, in

Say three short years, and crush the Man of Sin :

" Dear Lady Harvey ! this benighted land "—

" Ah, yes ! your trials we can understand . . .   300

" Those dreadful Priests "—" The cause of Scriptural

            Truth . . .

"Our Church in danger ... Government ... Maynooth"—

And leaving lovely damsels as they may

To quote *Evangeline, Traviata* play,

We move with Laurence on his homeward way. 305

   All down the leafy way as Bloomfield rode,

O'er man and horse the latticed moonshine flow'd,

Like films of sorcery, or sacred rite

Of sprinkling by the holy priestess, Night ;

Strange pools of mist were on the lower ground, 310

Moonlight above, and silence deep around,
Except the measured footfalls. In a shade
By thicker growths of laurustinus made,
Our young Squire heard not, or unheeding heard,
One whispering bough that stealthily was stirr'd ; 315
Saw not the glitter of an ambush'd eye
That glared upon the landlord moving by.
In meditation through the leaves he rode ;
O'er man and horse the web of moonshine flow'd ;
Then on the open highway swiftlier sped,   320
Where spectral gates and walls behind him fled.

Within, his soul was seething. Should he stay,—
Toil, wrangle, risk his blood, from day to day ?
Or from the tumult quietly withdraw,
And soon forget what he no longer saw ?   325
Was all his duty to his rental bound ?
Might he not better serve on other ground ?
It matters not for whom, or how, or where—
Be what you're fit for, all the world has share.

' These men are in their element, and do   330

' Much work ; it may be, are victorious too.

' Novels and newspapers alone afford

' Th' angelic peasant and his fiendish lord.

' Ev'n Duff has kindness ; Harvey's wit is small

' Yet leaves him average mortal after all ;   335

' Pigot is business-like and bold, not base,—

' One looks not there for Shelley's mind or face.

' Such have a manly spirit of their own,

' Which roughly in a rugged world is shown.

' And what know I of tenants or of land ?'—   340

Here conscience took once more the upper hand :

' Somewhat you know of men, and Heavenly Laws ;

' Permit not selfish sloth to win the cause ;

' The right choice wins a strength, wrong choice a plea.'

Perplex'd in mood, his mansion enters he,   345

With varying step along the lonely floors

And dismal dark neglected corridors.

A long discussion may, for good or ill,

Be sharply ended by despotic will.

' I'll quit the place before to-morrow night !   350

' Party with party, church with church may fight,

' Rich fools with poor,—I cannot set them right.'

But to the council-chamber of his head

Rush'd in a tale that he had long since redd,

An ancient story, putting all astray,   355

As Cæsar's self was stopt upon his way.

Imperial Hadrian, with his lofty knights,

Prancing through pillar'd gateway, Dion writes,

There saw a Widow kneeling to implore,

Since none could rescue save her emperor,   360

An audience of her suit ; to whom he said

" I have no time to hearken." Hope and dread

Together gone, she cried " Then cease to reign ! "

Whereat, amidst a check'd and wondering train,

The Roman wheel'd his horse and heard.   365

                                        This wrought

Another change of hue upon his thought.

' 'Twere hard to reign, to abdicate more hard.

' Is living free, like other men, debarr'd ?

' Shut eyes, and open (says the World) your
   mouth,

' And take what fortune sends you, foolish youth ! 370

' Would things go better here, supposing I,

' Not Pigot, govern'd ? ought I not to try ?

' Or are they dreams, my poetry and art,

' And love and faith too, all life's finer part—

' Fit but for conversation, books, the stage, 375

' And not for men whom actual toils engage ? '

His heart beat, and he felt as faint within

As one who has a whole day fasting been,—

Irresolution's sickness ; so combined

Are all the powers of body and of mind. 380

Moreover, looking on himself, he saw

A crisis of his life. *There* was Heaven's Law,

Cloudy, but firm and sure. He saw the crime

(Touching all future pleasures with a slime)

To stand before a true task face to face, 385

Then turn away, though secret the disgrace.

Man's life is double : hard its dues to give
Within, Without, and thus completely live.

    Custom of pray'r with wandering soul he kept ;
Desired to sleep, but not till daylight slept.   390

LAURENCE BLOOMFIELD IN IRELAND.

CHAPTER IV.

THE DORANS.

LAURENCE BLOOMFIELD

IN IRELAND.

IV.

THE DORANS.

JACK DORAN's cottage, from a bare hillside,   1

Look'd out across the bogland black and wide,

Where some few ridges broke the swarthy soil,

A patch of culture, won with patient toil.

The walls were mud, around an earthen floor,   5

Straw ropes held on the thatch, and by his door

A screen of wattles fenced the wind away,

For open wide from morn till dusk it lay,

A stool perhaps across, for barring out

The too familiar porker's greedy snout.   10

Thieves were undreamt-of, vagrants not repell'd,

The poor man's dole the pauper's budget swell'd,

A gift of five potatoes, gently given,
Or fist of meal, repaid with hopes of Heaven.

 There Jack and Maureen, Neal their only son, 15
And daughter Bridget, saw the seasons run ;
Poor but contented peasants, warm and kind,
Of hearty manners, and religious mind ;
Busy to make their little corner good,
And full of health, upon the homeliest food. 20
They tasted flesh-meat hardly thrice a-year,
Crock-butter, when the times were not too dear,
Salt herring as a treat, as luxury
For Sunday mornings and cold weather, tea ;
Content they were if milk the noggins crown'd, 25
What time their oatmeal-stirabout went round,
Or large potatoes, teeming from the pot,
Descended to the basket, smoking hot,—
Milk of its precious butter duly stript,
Wherewith to Lisnamoy young Biddy tripp'd. 30
Not poor they seem'd to neighbours poorer still,

As Doran's father was, ere bog and hill
Gave something for his frugal fight of years
'Gainst marsh and rock, and furze with all its spears,
And round the cottage an oasis green   35
Amidst the dreary wilderness was seen.
Two hardy cows the pail and churn supplied,
Short-legg'd, big-boned, with rugged horns and wide,
That each good spot among the heather knew,
And every blade that by the runnels grew,   40
Roved on the moor at large, but meekly came
With burden'd udders to delight the dame,
And in its turn the hoarded stocking swell'd
Which envious neighbours in their dreams beheld ;
At thought whereof were bumpkins fain to cast   45
Sheep's eyes at comely Bridget as she pass'd
With napkin-shaded basket many a morn ;
But every bumpkin Bridget laugh'd to scorn.

Who at an evening dance more blithe than she ?—
With steps and changes, modest in their glee,   50

So true she foots it, and so hard to tire,
Whilst Phil the Fiddler's elbow jerks like fire,
That courting couples turn their heads to look,
And elders praise her from the chimney-nook
Amidst their pipes, old stories, and fresh news.   55
From twenty decent boys might Bridget choose ;
For, put the jigs aside, her skill was known
To help a neighbour's work, or speed her own,
And where at *kemp* or *kayley* could be found
One face more welcome, all the country round ?   60
Mild oval face, a freckle here and there,
Clear eyes, broad forehead, dark abundant hair,
Pure placid look that show'd a gentle nature,
Firm, unperplex'd, were hers ; the Maiden's stature
Graceful arose, and strong, to middle height,   65
With fair round arms, and footstep free and light ;
She was not showy, she was always neat,
In every gesture native and complete,

kemp, a meeting of girls for sewing, spinning, or other work, ending
with a dance.
kayley, a casual gathering of neighbours for gossip.

Disliking noise, yet neither dull nor slack,
Could throw a rustic banter briskly back,   70
Reserved but ready, innocently shrewd,—
In brief, a charming flower of Womanhood.

The girl was rich, in health, good temper, beauty,
Work to be done, amusement after duty,
Clear undistracted mind, and tranquil heart,   75
Well-wishers, in whose thoughts she had her part,
A decent father, a religious mother,
The pride of all the parish in a brother,
And Denis Coyle for sweetheart, where the voice
Of Jack and Maureen praised their daughter's
          choice.   80
More could she ask for? grief and care not yet,
Those old tax-gatherers, dunn'd her for their debt ;
Youth's joyous landscape round her footsteps lay,
And her own sunshine made the whole world gay.

Jack and his wife, through earlier wedded years,   85

Untroubled with far-sighted hopes and fears,
Within their narrow circle not unskill'd ,
Their daily duties cautiously fulfill'd
Of house and farm, of bargain and of pray'r ;
And gave the Church and gave the Poor a share ;   90
Each separate gift by angels put in score
As plain as though 'twere chalk'd behind the door.
The two themselves could neither write nor read,
But of their children's lore were proud indeed,
And most of Neal, who step by step had pass'd   95
His mates, and trod the master's heels at last.

When manly, godly counsels took the rule,
And open'd to her young a freer school,
Poor Erin's good desire was quickly proved ;
Learning she loves, as long ago she loved.   100
The peasant, sighing at his own defect,
Would snatch his children from the same neglect ;
From house and hut, by hill and plain, they pour
In tens of thousands to the teacher's floor ;

Across the general island seems to come   105
Their blended voice, a pleasing busy hum.
Our little Bridget, pretty child, was there,
And Neal, a quick-eyed boy with russet hair,
Brisk as the month of March, yet with a grace
Of meditative sweetness in his face ;   110
To Learning's Temple, which made shift to stand
In cowhouse form on great Sir Ulick's land
(Who vex'd these schools with all his pompous might
Nor would, for love or money, grant a site),
Each morn with merry step they cross'd the hill, 115
And soon could read with pleasure, write with skill,
Amaze from print their parents' simple wit,
Decypher New-world letters cramply writ ;
But Neal, not long content with primers, redd
"Rings round him," as his mother aptly said ;   120
Sought far for books, devour'd whate'er he found,
And peep'd through loopholes from his narrow bound.

Good Maureen gazed with awe on pen and ink,

On books with blindest reverence. Whilst we think
The Dark and Middle Ages flown away,   125
Their population crowds us round to-day ;
So slowly moves the world. Our dame believed,
Firmly as saints and angels she received,
In witchcraft, lucky and unlucky times,
Omens and charms, and fairy-doctors' rhymes   130
To help a headache, or a cow fall'n dry ;
Strong was the malice of an evil eye ;
She fear'd those hags of dawn, who skimm'd the well,
And robb'd the churning by their May-day spell ;
The *gentle* race, whom youngsters now neglect,   135
From Mary never miss'd their due respect ;
And when a little whirl of dust and straws
Rose in her pathway, she took care to pause
And cross herself ; a twine of rowan-spray,
An ass's shoe, might keep much harm away ;   140
Saint Bridget's candle, which the priest had blest,
Was stored to light a sick-bed. For the rest,
She led a simple and contented life,

Sweet-temper'd, dutiful, as maid and wife ;
Her husband's wisdom from her heart admired,   145
And in her children's praises never tired.

 Jack was a plodding man, who deem'd it best
To hide away the wisdom he possess'd ;
Of scanty words, avoiding all dispute;
But much experience in his mind had root ;   150
Most deferential, yet you might surprise
A secret scanning in the small grey eyes ;
Short, active, though with labour's trudge, his legs ;
His knotted fingers, like rude wooden pegs,
Still firm of grip ; his breath was slow and deep ; 155
His hair unbleach'd with time, a rough black heap.
Fond, of a night, to calmly sit and smoke,
While neighbours plied their argument or joke,
To each he listen'd, seldom praised or blamed,
All party-spirit prudently disclaim'd,   160
Repeating, with his wise old wrinkled face,

" I never knew it help a poor man's case;"
And when they talk'd of "tyrants," Doran said
Nothing, but suck'd his pipe and shook his head.

In patient combat with a barren soil,   165
Jack saw the gradual tilth reward his toil,
Where first his father as a cottier came
On patch too poor for other man to claim.
Jack's father kept the hut against the hill
With daily eightpence earned by sweat and skill; 170
Three sons grew up ; one hasted over sea,
One married soon, fought hard with poverty,
Sunk, and died young ; the eldest boy was Jack,
Young herd and spadesman at his father's back,
With every hardship sturdily he strove,   175
To fair or distant ship fat cattle drove,
(Not theirs, his father had a single cow),
And cross'd the narrow tides to reap and mow.
A fever burn'd away the old man's life ;
Jack had the land, the hovel, and a wife ;   180

And in the chimney's warmest corner sat
His good old mother, with her favourite cat.

   Manus, now dead, (long since, on ' cottier-take,'
Allow'd cheap lodgment for his labour's sake)
Contriving days and odd half-days to snatch,   185
By slow degrees had tamed the savage patch
Beside his hut, driven back the stubborn gorse,
Whose pounded prickles meanwhile fed his horse,
And crown'd the cut-out bog with many a sheaf
Of speckled oats, and spread the dark-green leaf 190
Where plaited white or purple blooms unfold
To look on summer with an eye of gold,
Potato-blossoms, namely. Now, be sure,
A larger rent was paid ; nor, if secure
Of footsole-place where painfully he wrought,   195
Would Manus grumble. Year by year he sought
A safeguard ; but the Landlord still referr'd
Smoothly to Agent, Agent merely heard,
And answer'd—'We'll arrange it by and by ;

Meanwhile, you're well enough, man ; let it lie,'— 200
Resolved to grant no other petty lease,
The ills of petty farming to increase.
Old Manus gone, and Bloomfield's father gone,
Sir Ulick Harvey's guardian rule came on ;
And so at last Jack found his little all   205
At Viceroy Pigot's mercy, which was small.
With more than passive discontent he look'd
On tenacies like Jack's, and ill had brook'd
The whisper of their gains. He stood one day,
Filling the petty household with dismay,   210
Within their hut, and saw that Paudeen Dhu,
The bailiff, when he call'd it 'snug,' spoke true.

The patch'd, unpainted, but substantial door,
The well-fill'd dresser, and the level floor,
Clean chairs and stools, a gaily-quilted bed,   215
The weather-fast though grimy thatch o'erhead,
The fishing rods and reels above the fire,

Neal's books, and comely Bridget's neat attire,
Express'd a comfort which the rough neglect
That reign'd outside forbade him to expect. 220
Indeed, give shrewd old cautious Jack his way,
The house within had shown less neat array,
Who held the maxim that, in prosperous case,
'Tis wise to show a miserable face ;
A decent hat, a wife's good shawl or gown 225
For higher rent may mark the farmer down ;
Beside your window shun to plant a rose
Lest it should draw the prowling bailiff's nose,
Nor deal with whitewash, lest the cottage lie
A target for the bullet of his eye ; 230
Rude be your fence and field—if trig and trim
A cottier shows them, all the worse for him.
To scrape, beyond expenses, if he can,
A silent stealthy penny, is the plan
Of him who dares it—a suspected man ! 235
With tedious, endless, heavy-laden toil,
Judged to have thieved a pittance from the soil.

But close in reach of Bridget's busy hand
Dirt and untidiness could scarcely stand ;
And Neal, despite his father's sense of guilt,   240
A dairy and a gable-room had built,
And by degrees the common kitchen graced
With many a touch of his superior taste.

The peasant draws a low and toilsome lot ;
Poorer than all above him ?—surely not.   245
Conscious of useful strength, untaught to care
For smiling masquerade and dainty fare,
With social pleasures, warmer if less bland,
Companionship and converse nigh at hand,
If sad, with genuine sorrows, well-defined,   250
His life brought closer to a simpler mind ;
He's friends with earth and cloud, plant, beast and
          bird ;
His glance, by oversubtleties unblurr'd,
At human nature, flies not much astray ;
Afoot he journeys, but enjoys the way.   255

Th' instinctive faith, perhaps, of such holds best
To that ideal truth, the power and zest
Of all appearance; limitation keeps
Their souls compact; light cares they have, sound
   sleeps;
Their day, within a settled course begun,   260
Brings wholesome task, advancing with the sun,
The sure result with satisfaction sees,
And fills with calm a well-earn'd hour of ease.
Nay, gold, whose mere possession less avails,
Far-glittering, decks the world with fairy-tales. 265
Who grasp at poison, trigger, cord, or knife?—
Seldom the poorest peasant tires of life.

 Mark the great evil of a low estate;
Not Poverty, but Slavery,—one man's fate
Too much at mercy of another's will.   270
Doran has prosper'd, but is trembling still.
Our Agent's lightest word his heart can shake,
The Bailiff's bushy eyebrow bids him quake.

Jack had been urged, and thought the counsel good,
" Go, delve the prairie, clear the Western wood ; 275
There, with your little purse and vigorous arm,
Be king (for so you may) of house and farm."
But kindly to his native nook he clung,—
Too old his mother, and his babes too young,
His wife too timid,—till he found at last   280
His own brisk day for enterprise gone past,
And hoped with trembling, that, without a lease,
The LORD would let them pass their days in peace,
And leave the children settled well in life :
Such was the prayer of Doran and his wife.   285

School-teaching some, and some the Church advised
For Neal ; but Jack, from lifelong habit, prized
His hard-won and uncertain 'bit o' ground,'
And in his son's increasing vigour found
A welcome help, till soil and seasons claim'd   290
Neal's constant hand. But far too high it aim'd,

On house and field improvement bravely bent.
"My boy," said Jack, "you'll only *rise* the rent,
"Or get us hunted from too good a place,"—
And back'd his fears from many a well-known case. 295
He praised their added room, but shook his head,
The small new dairy fill'd his soul with dread,
To cut a drain might dig their own pitfall,
'Twas ostentation to rebuild a wall,
And did they further dare to stub the *whins*, 300
The Great-Folk soon would visit all their sins.
"We'll buy."—"But they won't sell."—"More ren
      we'll pay."

"They'll charge three prices, or snap all away."
What could Neal do?—his parents getting old,
Detain'd him; but his early hopes were cold. 305
Improve they must not; if permitted still
To merely stay, 'tis at their Agent's will.
They long have struggled, with some poor success,
But well they know, should harder fortunes press,

whins, gorse.

Their slow prosperity is thin and poor,   310
And may not even petty rubs endure.

From day to day th' unresting finger steals
Of Heaven's great clock, with all the stars for wheels,
Transmuting worlds, and every small thing too ;
The boy to man, the girl to woman grew ;   315
Jack stiffen'd; Maureen's hair was streak'd with white ;
The good old grandame vanish'd from their sight.
And day by day, on both estates, Jack sees
Old tenants losing place by slow degrees ;
No leases granted or renew'd ; the serf   320
Hemm'd from his former space of moor and turf ;
To grazing, here, the various tillage yields ;
There wide-spread farms absorb the petty fields ;
Gain, luxury, and love of power, inspire
New selfish schemes, that more and more require   325
All privilege and profit from the land
To rest completely in the Great-Folk's hand,
Accorded, changed, withheld, at their command.

Neal sometimes argues that, whilst yet in plight,

'Twere well to dare at last the distant flight.   330

" Let's go while go we may ; if things get worse

" They soon must leave us empty byre and purse.

" You're fresh, thank God, and lively, mother dear ;

" Father, we'd work and prosper well, no fear ;

" And rise to something, anywhere but here.   335

" There's Coyle, besides, in tiptoe haste to start ;

" One word, and Coyle is with us, hand and heart."

But age's caution, added to their own,

Still held the parents back from risks unknown.

One cool and grey autumnal night—the same 340

That sees Sir Ulick's banquet—round the flame

Of fragrant fir that branch'd a waving tree

Before the human form began to be,

And countless years lay sunk in black morass,

Are drawn this humble household. Slowly pass 345

Their quiet evening hours. If Maureen doze,

Her needles fail not, adding rows to rows

G

Of knitted wool; nor less untiring spins
Her daughter, who with skilful finger wins
The flowing yellow flax from rock to reel,   850
And chants a ditty to her murmuring wheel ;
The son and father bask, as well they may
Who handle flails as these have done to-day,—
The sweet-milk-and-potato supper done,
Their out-door creatures cared for, every one,   855
The cat and dog, too, comrades old and tried ;
In drowsy warmth reposing side by side.

    Jack thinks the times look bad. "God help the
        poor ! "
Sighs Maureen ; " We're not cowld or hungry sure,
" The Lord be praised !—but rising rints, *mavrone*, 360
" And failing crops, would soon scrape flesh from
        bone."
The girl had met a keeper, hung with grouse ;
She talks of banquet at the Moy *Big House :*
" They're at their dinner now,—and so polite,—

" With lovely dresses,—O to see the sight !"   365

" A glorious wish !"—arousing, mutters Neal,

" Though envy's pang he could not choose but feel.

" Our Landlord's on the start again, they say."—

" To us what matter, let him go or stay ?"—

" Well now," says Bridget, " he's a fine young man."

Her thoughts on Bloomfield's recent visit ran.   371

—" A gintleman o' plain discoorse, in troth,

" Good luck to him !" says Maureen. —" Chips and
        froth !"

Cries Neal : " I half began to speak my mind,

" But——." " All no use, no use, my son, you'd
        find.   375

" 'Twould only," Jack thinks, " drive our Agent mad."

The young man sat fire-gazing, sullen-sad.

    " Maychance you'd read us somethin', Nail
        asthore ?"—

The less 'twas understood, believed the more,

Her son's vast learning made Maureen rejoice ;   380

Her 'heart was aisy, listenin' to his voice.'
" Goin' out you are *avic?*   You won't be late ? "
" No, mother dear." They heard the garden gate
Clap loud behind him.   " He's across the hill
"To Ballytullagh,"—which but pleased them ill ; 385
This neighbouring hamlet being a noted place,
By Pigot, their Pashá, cast out from grace.

  Jack lit his pipe ; the mother deeply sigh'd ;
The girl in thought her humming spindle plied ;
Young Neal, the while, on glooming path, well-known,
That winds by clump of gorse and boulder-stone, 391
Mounted the ridge, and saw in shadowy skies
A red enormous moon begin to rise.

LAURENCE BLOOMFIELD IN IRELAND.

CHAPTER V.

BALLYTULLAGH.

LAURENCE BLOOMFIELD

IN IRELAND.

V.

BALLYTULLAGH.

The hamlet Ballytullagh, small and old,   1
Lay negligently cluster'd in a fold
Of Tullagh Hill, among the crags and moor ;
A windy dwelling-place, rough, lonesome, poor ;
So low and weather-stain'd the walls, the thatch   5
So dusk of hue, or spread with mossy patch,
A stranger journeying on the distant road
Might hardly guess that human hearts abode
In those wild fields, save when a smoky wreath
Distinguish'd from huge rocks, above, beneath,   10
Its huddled roofs.   A lane goes up the hill,

Cross'd, at one elbow, by a crystal rill,

Between the stepping-stones gay tripping o'er

In shallow brightness on its gravelly floor,

From crags above, with falls and rocky urns,   15

Through sward below, in deep deliberate turns,

Where each fine evening brought the boys to play

At football, or with *camuns* drive away

The whizzing *nagg;* a crooked lane and steep,

Older than broad highways, you find it creep,   20

Fenced in with stooping thorn-trees, bramble-brakes,

Tall edge-stones, gleaming, gay as spotted snakes,

With gold and silver lichen ; till it bends

Between two rock-based rough-built gable ends,

To form the street, if one may call it street,   25

Where ducks and pigs in filthy forum meet ;

A scrambling, careless, tatter'd place, no doubt ;

Each cottage rude within-doors as without ;

All rude and poor ; some wretched,—black and bare

And doleful as the cavern of Despair.   30

camuns, sticks bent at one end.   *nagg*, wooden ball.

And yet, when crops were good, nor oatmeal high,
A famine or a fever-time gone by,
The touch of simple pleasures, even here,
In rustic sight and sound the heart could cheer.
With voice of breezes moving o'er the hills,   35
Wild birds and four-foot creatures, falling rills,
Mingled the hum of huswife's wheel, cock-crow,
The whetted scythe, or cattle's evening low,
Or laugh of children. Herding went the boy,
The sturdy diggers wrought with spade and *loy*,   40
The tether'd she-goat browsed the rock's green ledge,
The clothes were spread to dry on sloping hedge,
The *colleens* did their broidery in the shade
Of leafy bush, or gown-skirt overhead,
Or wash'd and *beetled* by the shallow brook,   45
Or sung their ballads round the chimney-nook
To speed a winter night, when song and jest
And dance and talk and social game are best :
For daily life's material good enough

loy, a half-spade.   *beetling*, thumping clothes with a truncheon *(beetle)*.

Such trivial incidents and homely stuff.   50

Here also could those miracles befall

Of wedding, new-born babe, and funeral ;

Here, every thought and mood and fancy rise

From common earth, and soar to mystic skies.

This ancient Woman crown'd with snow-white hair,

With burden of a hundred years to bear,—   55

The marvels and enchanting hopes of youth,

The toil of life, and disappointing truth,

Delights and cares that wives and mothers know,

The turns of wisdom, folly, joy, and woe,   60

The gradual change of all things, year by year,

While she to one Great Doorway still draws near,

All good and ill from childhood to old-age,

For her have moved on this poor narrow stage.

A cottage built ; farm shifting hands ; big thorn 65

By midnight tempest from its place uptorn ;

The Church's rites, the stations, and the priests ;

Wakes, dances, faction-fights, and wedding-feasts ;

Good honest neighbours ; crafty wicked rogues ;
The wild youth limping back without his *brogues ;* 70
The money'd man returning from the West
With beard and golden watch-chains on his breast ;
He that enlisted ; she that went astray ;
Landlords and agents of a former day ;
The time of raging floods ; the twelve weeks' frost ; 75
Dear summers, and how much their oatmeal cost ;
The Tullagh baby-daughters, baby-sons,
Grown up, grown grey ; a crowd of buried ones ;
These little bygones Oona would recall
In deep-voiced Gaelic,—faltering now they fall,   80
Or on her faint lips murmur unaware ;
And many a time she lifts her eyes in pray'r,
And many an hour her placid spirit seems
Content as infant smiling through its dreams,
In solemn trance of body and of mind ;   85
As though, its business with the world resign'd,
The soul, withdrawn into a central calm,

brogues, rough shoes.

Lay hush'd, in foretaste of immortal balm.
—Secluded Ballytullagh, small, unknown,
Had place and life and history of its own.   90

  Great Pigot's wrath, which brought unnumber'd woes
On Ballytullagh's Muse of mine disclose !
These upland people, paupers as they were,
Retain'd almost an independent air,
Drawn from old times, for clearly could they trace 95
Long generations in the self-same place ;
Game-laws they scorn'd, and mearings on the moor,
And all new-fangled things could ill endure ;
Landlord and agent were their natural foes ;
Old custom for their simple guide they chose ;   100
All Pigot's plans appear'd to them unjust ;
They murmur'd ; and he only said, "You must !"
So, when he took away their mountain-run,
Enclosing half the heath for dog and gun,
And half to feed a stranger's herds and flocks,   105
A sturdy coarse disciple of John Knox,—

Sheep were soon missing, cattle night by night
Dock'd of their tails, hamstrung, or kill'd outright ;
The grazier too, at last, was waylaid, left
Of breath and blood and all but life bereft ;   110
And every witness question'd in the case
Mere falsehood swore, with calm unblushing face.

Pigot, and Pigot's bailiff, *Paudheen Dhu,*
Are still prepared for war, and like it too ;
Costs, fees, drop in, and profitable 'takes,'   115
While every change the rental higher makes,
Clears petty claims aside, a vexing swarm,
And brings estates to new and better form.
Herein Sir Ulick, for himself and ward,
Was soon with Pigot's plans in full accord ;   120
One half this upland being Sir Ulick's ground,
One half engirt by nephew Bloomfield's bound.
A day was fix'd, arrears must then be paid ;
For more police a tax on all was laid,—

Paudheen Dhu, Little Black Paddy.

New little barracks dropt in lonely spots   125

Where moping constables bewail'd their lots,—

For now the Ribbon-Snake was known to glide

With secret venom round this country-side ;

Till Tullagh Hill became a place accurst,

And Ballytullagh stood for blot the worst   130

On Magisterial map. In two year's time

The tranquil nook was grown a nest of crime,

A den of were-wolves to a landlord's sight ;—

And Pigot only ask'd for legal right.

Rich neighbouring farmers, noway ill-disposed,   135

Their cautious lips, if not their eyes, keep closed ;

They dread revenge, they dread the public shame

That clings and reeks around th' *informer's* name ;

For Ireland's long tradition, lingering yet,

Hath in two scales the Law, the People set.   140

Nay, Ribbonism keeps Landlordism in check :

They blame, they fear, but will not break its neck ;

To them belongs no sense of commonweal,

Authority as alien still they feel,

Ruled, without partnership or wholesome pride, 145

By Government that governs from outside.

Their native Church, where peasant sons might rise,

The rulers first despoil'd, and now despise.

Trade, wealth, flow elsewhere, why they cannot
 guess,

Save by constraint of ruling selfishness. 150

In their own narrow bound, the constant fight

For land goes on, with little ruth or right,

So far as they can see ; but every man

Takes all advantage that he safely can.

And so, as in the chamber of a mist 155

Moving as they move, sadly they persist,

And let the puzzling world be as it list.

Our Agent twice a year sent forth a show'r

Of Notices to Quit, and kept his power

Suspended *in terrorem :* now at length 160

Shall these atrocious tenants feel his strength.

On two or three a swift eviction falls,
And then on Pigot Captain Starlight calls,
High on the gatepost nailing up his card.
But sturdy Pigot perseveres: 'twere hard   165
If rampant ruffianism could overfrown
All right and rule, and grossly beat them down !
For desperate ill a desperate remedy.
Some suffer guiltless, that must always be ;
Ev'n in fair war the necessary blow   170
Sets distant hearts to weep ; but here the foe
From general sympathy his courage draws,
In that alone lies ambush'd from the laws.
A plain sharp lesson, read to all and each,
Is here the true and only way to teach.   175
Therefore let Ballytullagh's natives know,
In due and legal form, that—out they go.

The priesthood, meanwhile, gave its usual aid,
Fulfill'd its wonted rounds and duly pray'd,
Condoled in general words, and censured crime,   180

And watch'd with care the movements of the time.

For this alone its mystic flag unfurl'd—

The warfare of the Church against the World,

Each minor human interest has a claim

So far as mingling with the one great aim.   185

Imagination to the Church must cling,

A grand, accustom'd, venerable thing,

Which dignifies the chief events of life,

Securing Heav'n, avoiding vulgar strife ;

The more withdrawn from regions of dispute,   190

The more within its bounds made absolute ;

The citadel impregnably maintain'd,

So bit by bit may all the rest be gain'd.

Priests' characters are various—priests are men ;

The system single to a bird's-eye ken ;   195

The method changing with the world's events,

And still providing needful instruments,

Which may, as men, do nothing, bad or good,

And their own work have seldom understood.

Blame if you must, but scorn not, over-bold,   200

H

This Great Association, deep and old ;
With guidance for the wandering soul of man ;
Sure dogmas to believe, for those who can ;
One step, one blindfold step, and all goes right,
Your weakness guarded by celestial might.   205

This wide Kilmoylan Parish own'd the care—
Hills, plain, and town—of Father John Adair.
And Father Austin was his curate now,
A strong-built man of thirty, black of brow,
A silent man, with heavy jaws and chin,   210
Close-shaven, and a heavy soul within ;
You look, and guess him dangerous and deep,
Full of dark plans that make your flesh to creep,
A mine of mystic secrets ; but alas !
The narrow bounds he never may outpass   215
Constrict him, and it eats his heart to know
How short a way his seeming power can go.
The tedious years will slowly wear him tame,
Or else some channel for the smouldering flame

Give altar, platform, journal, one more voice   220
To bid the foolish, furious mob rejoice,
But those above him, on sharp watch to stand,
And gather up the reins with cautious hand.

  Adair the priest is bland and dignified;
The curate Austin sullen, sidelong-eyed;   225
Both do their office punctually and well,
And duly are revered; but, truth to tell,
The people, when their crimes they plan and plot,
Regard the blessed clergy scarce one jot.
Some few, the leading scoundrels and the worst, 230
Would laugh at Pio Nono if he curs'd;
From under conscience many slip aside,
Transgress, and somehow back to 'duty' glide;
While others meeting form with form (no more
Demanded), by interpretation's lore   235
And casuistry to equal Dens's own
Arrange what's best to be conceal'd and shown.

duty, observance of the rules of the Church, especially as to Confession.

From either side of that mysterious screen
Of plain fir-boards, in every chapel seen,
The usual whisper flows in much routine ;   240
It were not wise the suppliant soul to press
Which now, being there, is yielding, more or less ;
The Mother keeps on terms, can watch and wait,
Expecting full submission, soon or late,
And overlooking much, if, on the whole,   245
A man will not refuse to save his soul.
Life's daily details, counted great or small,
The Church absorbs and dominates them all,
Takes her own silent course with conscious might,
As earthly Judge Supreme of wrong and right,   250
To rule at last, in great and trivial things,—
The Servants' Servant grown to King of Kings.

Hot grew men's passions : golden harvest came
And ended : hotter wax'd this evil flame,
Turning all wholesome thoughts to dread and hate.
Jack to his own fireside kept close of late,   256

But Neal was not afraid to cross their hill
To Ballytullagh, welcomed with good-will,
When nightfall shadow'd mountain, moor, and glen,
To chat the girls and argue with the men,　　260
Or study in the *Firebrand*, Dublin print,
Seditious rhetoric and murderous hint.
Best scholar there, with skill and force he redd,
Explain'd, declaim'd, and on their flattery fed ;
Until at last, however unprepared,　　265
To lead an army would the Youth have dared.

One dismal Sunday morning, such a day
As brings the message, 'summer's past away,'
Neal with a sigh awoke ; nor when awake
Could free his bosom from a nameless ache,　　270
The misery of his slumber ; ill-content
Into the damp and sunless air he went.
The fowls, with stretching wings and eager screech,
Run up in vain his bounty to beseech ;
He rests his arms upon a wall, to gaze　　275

Across the scene, not sad in other days,

But now, all round, with dark and doleful hues

A sombre sky the sluggish bog imbues ;

Black pit and pool, coarse tuft and quaking
        marsh,

Stretch far away to mountains chill and harsh   280

Under the lowering clouds ; while, near at hand,

The waters grey in trench and furrow stand.

Beneath those mountains dim Lough Braccan lies,

A stream wherefrom to join the river hies,

Around their northern buttress bends a vale,   285

Where ocean's breath is blown in every gale,

And o'er the lake, far-seen from many a road,

Is Bloomfield's long-untenanted abode.

To Lisnamoy from Tullagh, either side,

Rough hills descend, and mingle with the wide   290

Grove-tufted, house-and-village-sprinkled plain ;

And far from north to south a roof of rain

Hangs heavily this morning ; dark and dead

The dismal view, and Neal's own heart like lead.

Call'd in to breakfast by a mother's care,　　295
His sister and himself for Mass prepare ;
But Mary is not well, and doubts the weather ;
She and her husband bide at home together.
Tranquil, at Neal and Bridget's pausing feet
(Yet there is discontentment's chosen seat)　　300
The little hamlet lies in sheltering bend,
Whereto with quicker steps they now descend ;
The sister carrying in a jug her boon
Of precious milk for sickly Rose Muldoon.

Inside the poorest hovel of the place,　　305
The seal of death was on a young girl's face,
' Far through in the decline,' beside whose bed
Her haggard father sat with drooping head ;
A neighbour woman, taking turn as nurse,
Upheld the sufferer when her cough grew worse. 310
"God save you, kindly. How is she to-day ?"
Then Rosy's feeble voice was heard to say,
" Is that you, Bridget darlin'?" White and thin

Her fingers rested clammily within
The other maiden's healthy palm ; death-bright　315
Her eyes met Bridget's, brimm'd with living light.
Bare grimy walls, a roof with many a flaw,
This corner strewn with turf, and that with straw,
A borrow'd bedstead, two old stools, no more,
To furnish round the damp uneven floor,　　　320
Three plates, three broken cups, an iron pot,
A batter'd black tin-porringer kept hot
Beside the gaping hearth, enough to choke
The unaccustom'd lungs with lazy smoke,—
Such was the house : yet Rose with many a tear　325
Implored "O not the Poorhouse, father dear !"
Quick with her broidery needle once was she,
The youngest and the busiest girl of three,
And now her father's last companion left ;
Long sickness had his home of every comfort reft.　330

Most of these peasants, (portion out the blame
Who can : on whom have such a rightful claim ?)

When all goes well, are one degree, no more,
From want; grim Hunger, always at the door,   334
With scarce a push comes in when aught goes wrong.
—Why hold their land? Why marry? Why this throng
Of naked children? Would you heap the rates
By help beyond the loathsome Poorhouse gates?
Why not take other work?—I tell you why:
There is no work: they needs must beg, or fly,   340
(O happy chance!) or else lie down and die.

Soon from each doorway issue comrades, drest,
Both 'boys and girls,' in humble Sunday best,
And all together, laughing, down the lane   345
They pick their steps, a smoother road to gain;
The trailing cloud has falling drops at edge,
But not enough to ask a sheltering hedge;
Discourse curtails the league to Lisnamoy,
And Bloomfield's doings many a tongue employ,
Till near the Town they draw, and each cross-road   350
Gives friendly increase to the moving crowd.

Old Father Flynn and his plain chapel walls
Are both no more ; from a great steeple calls
A bell that dins the rival church to shame,
And pseudo-gothic art asserts its claim   355
For pence and wonder in the unfinish'd pile,
A dull burlesque on mediæval style,
Stone nightmare, lumpish, set with eye and horn,
Of architectural indigestion born.
Roofless and ruin'd each old stately fane,   360
Or if a living voice in some remain,
The rich usurper's,—now on Irish skies
These new-born proofs of ancient faith arise.
Adair, the zealous, careful parish-priest,
Is gentle, smooth, and mild to man and beast,   365
With comely presence and colloquial skill,
Of secret thoughts, and cool tenacious will ;
An Irish mitre is perhaps his hope ;
A proper man for cardinal or pope.
Outside the Church, all teaching is a crime,   370
All strength diabolism : he bides his time

To gain at last the public purse for schools
In strict accordancy with holy rules ;
The dark unlawful oath he blames no less
Than Pigot ; all must One Great Power confess. 375
(What Power ?—enough ! each wandering thought
        suppress.)

He likes not England's rule, nor will he curse ;
The Church's children's ofttimes please him worse ;
Dark oaths and alien bonds are things of sin ;
Yet agitation doth concession win ;   380
He favours loyalty of much that kind
Which in a doubtful-temper'd dog you find,
That fawns and growls, obeys and shows his teeth,—
Servility with danger underneath ;
For so must selfish England understand   385
That Ireland is not wholly in her hand,
Yet want that old excuse to knit a frown,
Cry 'rebel !' and with fury smite her down.
Irish Republic ?—Irish Kingdom ?—none
Could less desire such thing beneath the sun   390

Than Father John Adair : your ship may roll,
But will you run her straight on rock or shoal
For mere impatience ? Of all men that live,
Such clerics are the most conservative ;
Perusing somewhat bitterly, no less,   395
Their map and daily roll-call of distress,
When scores around them, with the name of land,
Staring on hungry wife and children stand,
Unused by beggars' art to seek and shift,
And dreading from their only hold to drift.   400
To pay their clergy these are ill-prepared ;
The clergy's hard-won purse with them is often shared.

Between the Latin prayers the small quire sings;
In silence deep a tinkling handbell rings ;
The little altar-boys in white array   405
Kneel round the altar ; heads, black, fair, and grey,
Through all the crowded chapel, row on row,
Bow trembling and expectant : and with slow
And solemn gesture, mystic-robed, the Priest

Lifting the body and the blood of CHRIST,   410
Hath once again the miracle renew'd
Of that old sacrifice on Holy Rood.

  The Mass completed, all prepare to go ;
But hush ! the Father will not have it so.
He speaks ; th' arrested crowd is turn'd to stone ; 415
Familiar, but commanding, is his tone ;
The subject, Ribbonism ; and, word by word,
His fervour kindles, and his strength is stirr'd,
To caution, warn, implore, denounce, forbid.
"Think not," says he, "that what you plan is hid : 420
" The spy, the *stagg*, the traitor's at your heels !"
The straining throng its interest now reveals
By stirs and murmurs. " Picture, every one,
" Your husband, or your brother, or your son,
" March'd off to Carrick jail—" here women's cries 425
And och ! och ! och ! through all the building rise.
" Whisht ! hold your tongues ! attend to what I say !

stagg, informer.

" My children, shun the dark and dangerous way.

" Have any stray'd? let these, while yet there's
           time,

" Withdraw. To swear a wicked oath's a crime; 430

" To keep it, worse.   The Church, to whom is given

" All power to bind and loose in Earth and Heaven,

" Declares such oath is void, of no effect.

" And mark me well, you sinners that neglect

" This warning,—from God's altar I declare   435

" *You are not Catholics;* you cannot share

" The Holy Sacraments; and he that dies

" In this condition——" sobs and groans and cries

Ring through the chapel.

                      On their homeward way,

By reddening hedge, bare stubble, heather gay, 440

To distant hamlet, or thatch'd cottage lone,

Or through the street and byways of the town

(Some to the ruin'd abbey first repair,

Among its graves to breathe a special pray'r),

The scatter'd congregation closely sift   445

The reverend Father's lecture, and its drift.

Here are the sage remarks of Bill M'Cann,

Oracular and disputatious man,

Who, while he stitch'd and hammer'd at a shoe,

Would argue with the Pope, and 'sack' him too :— 450

" Some things a Parish Priest is bound to say.

" The clergy, mind you, have their game to play ;

" And whilst they always take the people's part,

" Keep in with powers that be,—no aisy art.

" Adair himself, Sir, has in private said   455

" That England gives us nothing but from dread ;

" And I myself heard Father Austin say,

" At Jack O'Reilly's door last market-day,

" 'Eject them all !—It's bad, and far too bad !

" No wonder if they drive our people mad ! ' "   460

And Curate Austin *was* at times too rash ;

He mourn'd the peasants' sufferings ; and the lash

Of Protestant contempt which made him sore,

sack, overcome in argument.

Impatiently, being young and proud, he bore.
Perhaps he said it,—and perhaps said more   465
In dingy room above the grocery shop,
No senior's eye his rhetoric to stop,
With Curate Michael of the neighbouring parish,
(He sole familiar there, and he was rarish,
Church keeping always, like a ship at sea,   470
Its hands all busy), quaffing dreary tea.
At least our Crispin Critic did not fail
To clap the Curate in th' opposing scale ;
And though the elder folk and womankind
Found this day's lecture greatly to their mind,   475
Young men and politicians, not a few,
Discussed the words, and freely blamed them too.
Among the rest our Neal and Denis talk'd,
Then both to Tullagh Hill with Bridget walk'd ;
A flask of holy water carrying she,   480
And Neal two ounces of the best black tea,
For Maureen. Though the miles were long and rough,
They seem'd to Denis short and smooth enough,

Nor cared he when the rain at nightfall flow'd
And made a torrent of his downward road,   485
A stout young cartman, whistling bold and gay,
Well used to vanquish weather and the way.
Priests,   Ribbonmen,   and   Landlords, — what   are
         these?

At every turn a girl's bright face he sees ;
Rich—poor—the dead unmeaning phrases !—Love 490
Is monarch, earthly kings how far above !

ɪ

LAURENCE BLOOMFIELD IN IRELAND.

CHAPTER VI.

NEAL AT THE LOUGH.

LAURENCE BLOOMFIELD

IN IRELAND.

CHAPTER VI.

NEAL AT THE LOUGH.

So fared it with the folk behind the hill   1
From Doran's—who did all his Agent's will,
And bade his son the same wise course pursue
But Neal had thoughts his father never knew.
Old Jack is cautious, as a beast that knows   5
His little burrow watch'd by natural foes;
But Neal is rash, and some there are who bring
To Pigot's Bailiff stories with a sting,
To seat themselves, perchance, in Doran's place,
Or at the least enjoy the Viceroy's grace.   10

Private and patriotic griefs combined
To trouble and perplex Neal's youthful mind.
At loose imagination's utmost pitch
He rates the powers and graces of the rich,
Not life in Saturn more beyond his grasp ;   15
And pictures, till the thought is like a wasp,
The narrow toils and hardships of the poor,
Which no kind hand assists them to endure ;
For rich and poor, contrasted lots at best,
Here plainly mean oppressors and opprest.   20
With this, Old Ireland's glories, and her wrongs,
Her famous dead, her landscapes, and her songs,
Were fever'd fancy's beverage,—things well known
Mingled with names and dreams confus'dly shown.
Poetic visions hover'd ; every page   25
For Erin's glory, every fireside sage
Whose *shanahus* a brooding audience drew,
Were pleasant to his soul, and gospel-true.
Since dumb her school-books upon Ireland's tale,

shanahus, old stories.

Other and looser teaching must prevail,   30
And ardent boyhood drink its greedy fill
Of every wild-sprung legendary rill
And holy fount—not in their virgin shade
So oft as lower channels, hot and clay'd.
But better thus, than dry and dusty live,   35
Devoid of all th' ancestral past can give,
And every human touch from hill and shore
Being blotted out, let memory claim no more
In this her ancient realm, than where, exiled,
The shepherd sadly tracks th' Australian wild.   40

By fits, moreover, hide them as we may,
It frets us all, this tedious every-day ;
A longing throb, a germ of bold romance,
Is deep in every bosom ; thirst for chance
And change, and rich adventure. Sadly brave   45
This sends us wandering on the dismal wave,
Or earth's remotest mountains ; this gives war
Its frenzied life, and stirs more crime by far

Than moralist or lawyer ever guess'd ;
Soul-fermentation, anxious blind unrest,   50
That, sick of all the barren hours afford,
Will seize on dice, the tankard, or the sword ;
Or burst its limits in a headlong flood,
A mingling overflow of fire and mud,
To do a deed,—of glory, or of shame,   55
As outward things take hue from vulgar fame.
To this unquiet, lawless, dangerous mood,
The present seems a prison-house ; all good
(Though mainly shadows from our fancies cast)
Being in the boundless future, boundless past ;   60
Great things that have been, greater things to be ;
As if a man could, save in soul, be free.

Neal fain would join that secret brotherhood,
The rich men's terror ; but his father shrewd,
Who saw the 'Ninety-eight, and blamed alike   65
The yeoman's pitch-cap, and the rebel's pike,
Whose earliest memories were of houses burning,

Dead men from branches hung, and slowly turning,

Jack oft admonish'd him ; and on her knees

Maureen implored her son from thoughts like these. 70

Yet still he hanker'd for the fruit forbid :

A thousand gliding scenes the curtain hid

Of plot profound, and daring enterprise ;

And he himself, acknowledged brave and wise,

Head of the mystic band was seen to rise.   75

Great, too, this charm of mystery ; to swear,

Fling stealthy signs, enchant the common air.

When whispering schoolboys to a corner creep,

Bedim their shallow plans and call them deep,

Whilst uninitiates vainly pry and dodge,   80

Behold in bud the sacred cryptic lodge,—

For evil or for good, a power confess'd

In that old east, as in our modern west.

To check the tyrant Rich ; perchance to see

His injured country 'glorious, great, and free';   85

To help 'the patriot cause' with heart and hand ;
So Neal aspired ; and all was vague and grand.

  Not always prisoner by the dull bog-side
Was he ; not always heavy skies abide.
Among those mountain-skirts a league away   90
Lough Braccan spread, with many a silver bay
And islet green ; a dark cliff, tall and bold,
Half-muffled in its cloak of ivy old,
Bastion'd the southern brink, beside a glen
Where birch and hazel hid the badger's den,   95
And through the moist ferns and firm hollies play'd
A rapid rivulet from light to shade.
Above the glen, and wood, and cliff, was seen,
Majestically simple and serene,
Like some great soul above the various crowd,   100
A purple mountain-top, at times in cloud
Or mist, as in celestial veils of thought,
Abstracted heavenward.

                  Creeps a little boat,

Along the path of evening's golden smile,

To where the shatter'd castle on its isle   105

May seem a broad-wing'd ship; two massive tow'rs

Lifted against the yellow light that pours

On half the lough and sloping fields,—half-laid,

Creek, bush, and crag, within the mountain shade.

Dark bramble-leaves now show a curling fringe, 110

And sallies wear the first autumnal tinge;

With speckled plumes high wave the crowded reeds,

Amongst whose watery stems the mallard feeds.

Full many a time, on deep Lough Braccan's wave,

Has Neal inveigled from its liquid cave,   115

With youthful comrades, in a fragile keel,

The pike, the perch, the trout, the twisting eel;

Alone, and musingly, he glides to-day,

Has fish'd an hour in vain, and coil'd his line away.

The coble beach'd at lonely Innisree   120

High at a rifted window, musing free

' sallies,' or sallows (*salix.*)

On ancient sky and water, freshly fair,

A poet's or a painter's rich despair,

And on the fame of olden times, which threw

Across the firm world a transcendent hue,   125

No more with petty toils and cares dismay'd,

The young man watch'd that glowing landscape fade.

South-westward, where th' autumnal sun went down,

A lake-reflected headland heaved its crown

Of darkling trees, and, knew you where to search,   130

The hoary ruins of a little church,

That mingled there with human skulls and bones

The mossy downfall of its sculptured stones ;

While, like one poem scatheless and sublime

Amid the vast forgetfulness of Time,   135

Slender and tall a Round Tower's pointed crest

Rose dimly black against the gorgeous west.

Methinks I stand with Neal, and, wide-eyed, gaze

Far through the wondrous world of former days.

In clear-obscure extends th' Ogygian Isle,   140
Deep-forested, but lit with many a smile
Of lake and river, and empurpling air,
The mantle of its mountains; wolf and bear
In rocky cave and wild-wood shadow skulk;
Free rove the stag and heavy-headed elk;   145
Broad plain and valley spread their brilliant green,
With pathless fen and sombre moor between;
The changeful waste of ocean circling all;
Whose tides in frith and channel flow and fall
To dance the wild man's curragh,—till, some day,   150
Poops of strange wing are gliding up his bay;
An era, whilst he stares with dread and wonder,
Closes its portals, without crash of thunder;
Portals to us (yet sun and moon were bright)
That seem the barriers of a realm of night.   155
At history's dawn, the sons of the great east,
Gigantic, spectral, doubtful, move in mist,
Old Afric, Scythic, or Phenician fames,

' curragh,' or coracle, a little boat of hide stretched on wicker.

Nemidians and Fomorians, dusky names,
Firbolgs, Danaäns, and Milesians proud,—   160
Fair shadowy queens, like floating forms of cloud,
With rugged Kings, Druids white-raimented,
A thin gold crescent on each awful head,
Sage Brehons, Bards, and Minstrels ; and a roar
Of battles, like a sea on distant shore,   165
Sounds from the mighty hollow of the Past.

   Let the huge stones be desolate ; the last
Man's blood smoke up to Crom.   That solemn night
Of Beltane, when King Layorie's hand must light
The mystic blaze on Tara first of all,   170
Behold on distant hill, at twilight-fall,
A fire,—for which the penalty is death.
Whilst frowning Druids pour prophetic breath,
Spears bring the malefactor ; on whose face
Of heavenly calm, doth every prince in place   175
Mute-wondering stare, until with awe-struck sense

'Crom,' a pagan deity.

Horc, son of Dego, bows in reverence

Before SAINT PATRICK. Slave, he herded swine

In Dalaradia once ; the will divine,

By messengers at midnight when he dream'd,   180

Bade him return to Ireland, and it seem'd,

At Tours within Saint Martin's cloister-wall,

He heard the voices of the Irish call,—

'We pray thee come to us !'

O loving, mild,

And docile people !—as to parent, child,   185

To Patrick, Bridget, fearless Columbkill,

Knelt all the land. 'Their bones one grave do fill.'

A luckless land at length ; a grave much wrong'd.

Meantime, for learning and religion throng'd

All Europe to the furthest western isle,   190

With many a studious and monastic pile

Thick-sown, and many a blessed man she sent

To bring the souls of people nourishment

In kingdoms far away.

But ships came forth

For plunder, from the pagan pirate North,   195
Who tore this isle ; and these were not the worst.
Dermot MacMurrough, be thy name accurst !
And, wert thou Pope (as Pope thou wast indeed),
Thine, Nicholas Breakspeare ! who to Norman greed
Sold what to neither could belong of right.   200
Strongbow, De Courcy, many a mail-clad knight,
Drive in the wedge of steel with stalwart blows ;
Vainly the saffron-shirted kerns oppose
With axe and sling, their feet and bosoms bare,
No helmet but their matted glibbs of hair ;   205
Vain the swift javelin, vain the furious rush
On bareback'd horses from deep woods, to crush
The Sassenach ; slow lives of plotting pain,
Outbursts of fever'd frenzy, all are vain,
King Brian he is dead, who smote the Dane.   210

Alas, no bond the troubled chieftains know
To weld their strength against the common foe ;

'glibb,' the natural hair grown in a thick mass.

Each power in turn promoted and suppress'd,
Through Desmond, Thomond, Brefney, and the West.
Edwards and Henrys waste the land by turns,   215
The bloated king her ancient worship spurns,
Entrench'd within the fortress of her frill
His sour-faced daughter works her shrewish will,
Cajoles or strikes, unpitying, to destroy
Fraternal patriotism, her worst annoy.   220
Ultonia last its undulating fields
And dark-blue mountains to th' invader yields;
From far Tyrconnell, like a northern gale,
O'Donnell sweeps upon the English Pale;
O'Neill defends the passes of Tyrone;—   225
Last of the princes, these are also gone.

Let pedant James now part the plunder'd lands,
And chaffer out his bag of Bloody Hands;
Let slippery Charles depute his squire, Black Tom;
The blacker 'Curse of Cromwell' spread its gloom; 230
From Orange William sneaking Shemus fly,

K

And brave men for a coward vainly die ;
Where slaughter ends let treachery begin ;
Ireland must lose, no matter who may win ;
Derided in her torture and her tears,   235
In sullen slavery dragging hopeless years ;
Of social ties mere cruel scourges made ;
A ban upon her learning and her trade ;
Possessions, rights, religion, language, torn
And crush'd by Law—a word to hate and scorn 240
For those taught English in oppression's school,
And reading good words by the witches' rule ;
A name for powerful wrong, with no appeal ;
Since law at every moment made them feel
To live an Irishman on Irish ground   245
The sole unpardonable crime was found.

Island of bitter memories, thickly sown
From winding Boyne to Limerick's treaty-stone,
Bare Connaught Hills to Dublin Castle wall,
Green Wexford to the glens of Donegal,   250

Through sad six hundred years of hostile sway,

From Strongbow fierce to cunning Castlereagh!

These will not melt and vanish in a day.

These can yet sting the patriot thoughts which turn

To Erin's past, and bid them weep and burn.   255

   The dusk has gather'd, vapour chill unfurls

Down all the mountain-height, and creeps and curls

Along the glens and edges of the lake,

Like slumber on a mind still half-awake;

While round the small and broken winding-stair 260

In the wall's thickness, Neal descends with care,

And stooping through the pointed arch below

Is strongly seized by some expectant foe.

He struggles hard, his elbows pinion'd tight,

Bursts up, and writhes, and strains with all his

       might;   265

Till now the hat from his assailant flies,

And shows Tim Nulty's merry-twinkling eyes,

A Ribbonman of note, who oft has fill'd

The stripling's ear with flattery not unskill'd.

"Yourself, man !—searchin' for the pot o' gold ? 270

"By japers, you're no aisy bird to hold !

"'Tis you, Nail, not a spy,—I'm glad to see it.

"Luck's in our meeting : now or never be it !"

Tall, in the shadow of the ruin, stood

A silent Stranger, draped in cloak and hood.   275

"Sir, I have heard of you !"—he took Neal's hand ;

"We count on you to join our patriot band."

"I'll join, sir !"—"On the minute ?"—"Yes !"—

   "Well said !—

"Doran, there's powerful interest at our head,

"As by degrees you'll know,—but that must wait. 280

"I'm from the Grand Lodge, County Delegate.

"Hats off ! grip tight the Gospels !—now attend,

"And word for word say with me, to the end :

 "'I swear by the Most Holy Trinity

 "'A true and faithful Ribbonman to be ;   285

"'To do my best to strike off England's chain;

"'The poor against the rich man to sustain;

"'Ever to help and never to betray

"'My brethren; my superiors to obey

"'At all times, without question or delay,   290

"'Pity or mercy. If I break this oath,

"'Destruction seize my soul and body both!

"'Amen, by kiss! Amen, by cross! Amen!'

"Here is your card. To-morrow night at ten.

"The place Shawn Roe's. *King Malachi* the pass." 295

"Now come," the other says, "one christnin' glass.

"Brother, your noble health!—You've done what's
        right.

"There's more to tell you, Neal, to-morrow night.

"We'll then admit, in form and order due;

"And proud the boys will be, at sight of you." 300

Both boats lay dark where ivy-trailers hid

A little cavern, whence the coble slid

Into the dim expansive lough, and broke

Its hush'd and starry dream with rippling stroke,
No other sound between the earth and sky   305
Save rom the misty shore, the plover's cry.

But shortening days that flit on silent wing
Near and more near the fate of Tullagh bring.
Has Pigot shown relentment? "Out they go!"
Says Pigot, and will keep his tryst they know. 310
When Bloomfield sought to move his uncle's mind,
'Twas vainly : "Pigot's views are right, you'll find.
"Pigot has vast experience—thirty years'.
"No wise man with his agent interferes
"At such a crisis ; strengthen well his hands, 315
"Good sense advises, honour too demands.
"Your trusty general, with the foe in face,
"Would you, on little cause or none, disgrace?
"This is no time—" "But *foe*," said Laurence, "why?"
—"Such is the world," Sir Ulick made reply, 320
"At least in Ireland here: I wish I knew
"Much less about it : how I envy you!"

LAURENCE BLOOMFIELD IN IRELAND.

CHAPTER VII.

TENANTS AT WILL.

LAURENCE BLOOMFIELD

IN IRELAND.

VII.

TENANTS AT WILL.

THE steady world pursued its common way
Yet some good luck, before that evil day,
Might intercept the hand outstretch'd to tear
Those cottage roofs, and leave their hearthstones bare.
If coming ills be distant half a mile,   5
Poor Paddy can forget, and gaily smile,
From carelessness, or fatalism, or sense
Profound of overruling Providence.

  But Pigot's ruddy cheek and sharp black eye
Display no softer hint, as months go by;   10

And now the trembling tenants whisper sad,—

" O Queen of Heaven! and would he be so bad?

" And will they send us begging, young and old,

" And seize the fields, and make the firesides cold,

" Where, God's our witness, poor enough we live, 15

" But still content with what the Lord may give,

" Our hearts with love and veneration tied

" To where our fathers' fathers lived and died?"

Or else more fiercely,—" 'Tis our native land!

" But cruel tyrants have us at command,   20

" To let us grow, if best it serves their needs,

" Or tear and cast us forth like poison-weeds.

" The law's their implement: who make the law?

" The rich men for the rich, and leave no flaw.

" And what's the poor man's part? to drudge and

          sweat   25

" For food and shelter. Does the poor man get

" Bare food and shelter?—praties, cabin, rags.

" Now fling him out to famish—or he drags

" His weary body to that gaol and grave

" The Poorhouse ;—he must live and die a slave, 30

" Toil, starve, and suffer, creep, and crouch, and crawl,

" Be cursed and trampled, and submit to all,

" Without one murmur, one rebellious trace

" Among the marks of misery on his face !"

Each tongue around old Oona feared to tell   35

The great misfortune, worse than yet befell

In all her length of journey. When they tried

To move her—"Would they take her life ?" she cried ;

At which it rested, hap what happen might.

And scarcely one, in truth, prepared for flight ;   40

Contempt of prudence, anger, and despair,

And *vis inertiæ*, kept them as they were ;

" God and the world will see it,"—so they said,

" Let all the wrong be on the doer's head !"

In early morning twilight, raw and chill,   45

Damp vapours brooding on the barren hill,

Through miles of mire in steady grave array

Threescore well-arm'd police pursue their way ;
Each tall and bearded man a rifle swings,
And under each greatcoat a bayonet clings ;   50
The Sheriff on his sturdy cob astride
Talks with the Chief, who marches by their side,
And, creeping on behind them, Paudeen Dhu
Pretends his needful duty much to rue.
Six big-boned labourers, clad in common frieze,   55
Walk in the midst, the Sheriff's staunch allies ;
Six crow-bar-men, from distant county brought,—
Orange, and glorying in their work, 'tis thought,
But wrongly,—churls of Catholics are they,
And merely hired at half-a-crown a day.   60

The Hamlet clustering on its hill is seen,
A score of petty homesteads, dark and mean ;
Poor always, not despairing until now ;
Long used, as well as poverty knows how,
With life's oppressive trifles to contend.   65
This day will bring its history to an end.

Moveless and grim against the cottage walls
Lean a few silent men : but some one calls
Far off ; and then a child 'without a stitch'
Runs out of doors, flies back with piercing screech, 70
And soon from house to house is heard the cry
Of female sorrow, swelling loud and high,
Which makes the men blaspheme between their teeth.
Meanwhile, o'er fence and watery field beneath,
The little army moves through drizzling rain ;   75
A 'Crowbar' leads the Sheriff's nag ; the lane
Is enter'd, and their plashing tramp draws near ;
One instant, outcry holds its breath to hear ;
" Halt !"—at the doors they form in double line,
And ranks of polish'd rifles wetly shine.   80

The Sheriff's painful duty must be done ;
He begs for quiet—and the work's begun.
The strong stand ready ; now appear the rest,
Girl, matron, grandsire, baby on the breast,
And Rosy's thin face on a pallet borne ;   85

A motley concourse, feeble and forlorn.
One old man, tears upon his wrinkled cheek,
Stands trembling on a threshold, tries to speak,
But, in defect of any word for this,
Mutely upon the doorpost prints a kiss,   90
Then passes out for ever. Through the crowd
The children run bewilder'd, wailing loud ;
Where needed most, the men combine their aid ;
And, last of all, is Oona forth convey'd,
Reclined in her accustom'd strawen chair,   95
Her aged eyelids closed, her thick white hair
Escaping from her cap ; she feels the chill,
Looks round and murmurs, then again is still.

Now bring the remnants of each household fire ;
On the wet ground the hissing coals expire ;   100
And Paudeen Dhu, with meekly dismal face,
Receives the full possession of the place.

Whereon the Sheriff, " We have legal hold.

" Return to shelter with the sick and old.

" Time shall be given ; and there are carts below   105

" If any to the workhouse choose to go."

A young man makes him answer, grave and clear,

" We're thankful to you ! but there's no one here

" Going back into them houses : do your part.

" Nor we won't trouble Pigot's horse and cart."   110

At which name, rushing into th' open space,

A woman flings her hood from off her face,

Falls on her knees upon the miry ground,

Lifts hands and eyes, and voice of thrilling sound,—

" Vengeance of God Almighty fall on you,   115

" James Pigot !—may the poor man's curse pursue,

" The widow's and the orphan's curse, I pray,

" Hang heavy round you at your dying day ! "

Breathless and fix'd one moment stands the crowd

To hear this malediction fierce and loud.   120

Meanwhile (our neighbour Neal is busy there)

On steady poles be lifted Oona's chair,

Well-heap'd with borrow'd mantles ; gently bear
The sick girl in her litter, bed and all ;
Whilst others hug the children weak and small 125
In careful arms, or hoist them pick-a-back ;
And, 'midst the unrelenting clink and thwack
Of iron bar on stone, let creep away
The sad procession from that hill-side gray,
Through the slow-falling rain. In three hours
      more   130
You find, where Ballytullagh stood before,
Mere shatter'd walls, and doors with useless latch,
And firesides buried under fallen thatch.

The Doran household, shadow'd with dismay,
Can still perform a pious part to-day ;   135
Jack Doran's mother, now deceased a year,
Was Oona's cousin ; Oona's welcomed here ;
Nor will her grandson in his duty fail,
Though now across the sea compell'd to sail.

" Man, woman, child,—they're gone, dear !" Mary
                said,   140

" And here we sit and mourn them like the dead.

" It falls like death, as cowld upon the heart,

" For kin and kindly neighbours thus to part.

" There won't be one face left we used to know,

" Not one companion out of long-ago.   145

" The good oul' people !—why should this befall ?

" Och, *murneen* boys and girls, where are ye all ?

" Through the wide world they're scatter'd, *fareer
                gair !*

" Sarch for them, barrin' Ireland, everywhere.

" Sure Ireland once was blest,—and was she curst 150

" Since then ? or what has made her last and
                worst ?

" The Heretics that robb'd the Church, some say :

" But glory be to God, amin, this day !"—

For gentle Maureen seldom said so much ;

And this was theme too perilous to touch.   155

murneen, darling.   *fareer gair !* bitter grief !

So was the little Hamlet's crowd at last
Whirl'd off like leaves before misfortune's blast.
Some from a seaport, and their lot the best,
On Neptune's Highway follow'd, east or west,
The myriads of their kindred gone before,—   160
If Irish still, yet Ireland's nevermore.
Some wander'd through the country; some went
          down,
Like Rose, to back-lane lodgings in the Town ;
And some to those high-built repulsive walls
Where Doctor Larmour paid his daily calls.   165
Dispensary and workhouse own'd his care,
An Antrim Presbyterian, short and spare,
Quick, busy, cool ; with lancet or with pill
Acknowledged first in Æsculapian skill.
Catholicism he openly despised,   170
But ailing Papists cleverly advised,
And men of every creed his talent prized.
Him Bloomfield knew. For Ballytullagh's fall
The Doctor's pity, Bloomfield found, was small.

" They lived in filth, perpetual sickness bred,   175

" Lazy of hand, and obstinate of head ;

" Gave rent too much for all they really made,

" Being well-nigh savage in the farming trade,

" Too small for what they wasted and o'erran.

" At risk of bloodshed let another plan   180

" Improvement, lawful owner though he be,—

" Mere owner ! what the devil right has he ?

" Poorer, of course, they could not fail to grow ;

" But humble, willing to be taught ? O no !

" See vice and crime and folly now array'd   185

" Conspirators, in ragged masquerade ;

" *Erin-go-bragh !*—yet, scoundrels ten times worse,

" And more deserving the true patriot's curse

" Than these poor scurvy rogues, are some who claim

" With public voice the patriot's lofty name ;   190

" That *mimber*, soaring on the rabble's yell ;

" This journalist, his rotten page to sell ;

" Or briefless barrister, whose frantic word,

" A cry for victuals, must and will be heard.

" Ireland, forsooth, 'a nation once again !'   195

" If Ireland was a nation, tell me when ?

" For since the civil modern world began

" What's Irish History ?   Walks the child a man ?

" Or strays he still perverse and immature,

" Weak, slothful, rash, irresolute, unsure ;   200

" Right bonds rejecting, hugging rusty chains,

" Nor one clear view, nor one bold step attains ?

" What Ireland might have been, if wisely school'd,

" I know not : far too briefly Cromwell ruled.

" We see the melting of a barbarous race,   205

" Sad sight, I grant, sir, from their ancient place ;

" But always, everywhere, it has been so ;

" Red-Indians, Bushmen, Irish,—they must go !"

The Doctor harshly spoke ; yet did his best

To cure the sick, and comfort the distress'd ;   210

And tended Rosy kindly,—to whose aid

A rill of Bloomfield's bounty he convey'd.

Those, too, with less to spare, and those with
         nought,
To this poor girl their friendly succour brought.
Here in a neighbouring house, but whence no noise 215
Can reach her, some well-wishing girls and boys
Have clubb'd their moneys, raffling for a shawl ;
Of Rose's other shreds the pawn has all.
Three simple pence entitle to a throw ;
Down on a slate the names and numbers go ;   220
The wooden cubes mark'd with a red-hot wire
(No better dice or dice-box they require)
In old tin porringer flung rattling fast,
A warmer interest watches every cast ;
" Follie' your han' !"   " You're lucky, throw for
         me !"   225
" More power !"   "Tim Ryan has it—fifty-three !"
Then silver, copper, mix'd, a bulky pound
Makes haste to Rosy, feebly turning round
With grateful smile ; and back the shawl comes too,
The winner swearing 'twas for her he threw.   230

Meanwhile, no raffle ends without a dance :
My boy, choose out a partner, and advance
To ask the fiddler for her favourite tune,
Slipping into his hand the penny boon ;
Polthoge, or *Washerwoman*, let him play,   235
Heart of my Kitty, or *The Fields in May ;*
She makes a pretty quibbling with her toes,
But he his agile power untiring shows
In many a double-shuffle, stamp and fling ;
Nor slack in praises are the crowded ring,—   240
" Success to both !—my boul' you wor' !—ay *that !*
" Don't spare him, Peggy dear !—Hurroo for Pat !"
They meet, change sides, the rapid steps renew,
A second wind inspires the fiddler too,
Till *Colleen Dhas*, well-flush'd in cheek, but grave 245
As courtly dames in minuets behave,
Signals ; when hand in hand the two give o'er,
Bow to the music, and resign the floor ;
Where other pairs achieve with equal zeal
The busy jig, or winding four-hand reel.   250

The dance-house, all the better for being bare,
Its broken roof admitting fresher air,
This poor and merry company befits ;
With jest and mimicry and clash of wits
Con 'Pastime' keeps them laughing long and loud ; 255
Sweethearts draw close together in the crowd ;
Gay groups of damsels, gather'd near the door
Banter to death each awkward bachelor,
And dart some flying jokes at Denis Coyle,
Whose travell'd wit such weapons well can foil, 260
For, do their utmost, Denis will not dance,
And slips away upon the earliest chance.

But all is not amusement. Near to these
Stands one at watch ; and ever when he sees
A man expected, pushing through the line, 265
By look or touch conveys a rapid sign.
As Denis goes, the grip salutes his hand
Which greets a Brother of the Midnight Band ;
And soon the whisper none may safely slight

Commands his presence on to-morrow night   270
With hour and place ; for Neal and Denis both
Have sworn the Ribbonman's unlawful oath.

   The dark and lonely street young Denis treads,
With mind confused, and fill'd with shapeless dreads ;
Where Doctor Larmour's lamp shoots forth a ray,   275
He shuns the light, and slinks across the way.

LAURENCE BLOOMFIELD IN IRELAND.

CHAPTER VIII.

A RIBBON LODGE.

LAURENCE BLOOMFIELD

IN IRELAND.

VIII.

A RIBBON LODGE.

At Lisnamoy, my friendly reader, deign   1
To pick your steps along a narrow lane,
And stop at Matthew Gorman's dirty door.
A sow is lodger upon Mat's ground-floor,
And grunts a welcome; follow me with care,   5
I'll guide you up the dark, the shaky stair;
And here is Matthew's schoolroom,—rather say
It was, for now its glory's past away,
Though still a night-school struggles to exist
For boys of larger growth, a bearded list.   10
Not merely copybooks are written there,

Not much for reading do the students care,

Except the *Firebrand*, redd aloud by Mat,

A lazy, pompous man, unclean, and fat ;

And oft goes round, when learning proves too dry, 15

A jar that never met the gauger's eye.

Big is the hearth, the fire is mostly small,

Rough desks and benches range along the wall,

The panes are patch'd with inky leaf and clout ;

A useful though unsavoury pile without   20

May help again, as it has help'd before,

Retreat more quick and private than by door,

'Mong filthy narrow yards and tumbling walls.

To Matthew's house to-night, as twilight falls,

With passwords, from the lane, and grip of hand, 25

By ones and twos arrive a secret band,—

" Where are you from ?" " South-aist." " The night
        is dark."

" A star will shortly rise."   " You know the mark ?"

" Milesius must be ready."   " What's your sign ?"

" *Lamh dearg an oughter !*" " *Tubbermore* is mine : 30
" Pass, brother." Past the sow, and up the stair,
They grope through darkness into ruddy glare,
The two old grimy windows, looking back,
Being curtain'd for the nonce with plies of sack.
The Lodge is filling fast ; in various groups 35
Lounge Captain Starlight's famed and dreadful troops ;
Two score in count at last, the most of whom
Are young and brainless, fill the stifling room.

Beside the door, a knot of ' labourin'-boys,'
The farmer these, and those the squire employs, 40
Yawn wide and mope, till whiskey in their brain
Kindle its foolish fire, with flashes vain
Wrapt in dull smoke, to send them blundering back
O'er field and fence upon their homeward track.
From outhouse loft, at need, or barnfloor bed, 45
The clumsy body and the stupid head

Lamh dearg an oughter, the red hand uppermost.
Tubbermore, the Great Well (name of a place).

Escape, with matchbox, or with stick in fist,
To burn or batter as their leaders list,
With knife to maim the cows, or loaded gun
To rake a peaceful window, and to run.   50

  A broken tradesman's aspect of disgrace,
Torn coat, big eyes, and pale unwashen face,
Shrink in a corner.   Bold sits Bill McCann,
The keen, small, wither'd, disputatious man,
With spectacles on nose, and quid in jaw,   55
Ready to argue histh'ry, po'thry, law,
Religion, science, or the latest news.
Bill earns his frugal crust by making shoes ;
Debate his recreation,—most of all
With 'Lordy' Mullan glad to try a fall.   60
But now to *Dublin Firebrand* Bill gives heed,
As Mat in solemn voice goes on to read :
" Who plotted for a famine ? who was gay
" To see the Celtic millions melt away,

'Lordy,' a hunchback.

" Foodless and fever'd; while their native soil   65

" Outpour'd the wealthy produce of their toil?

" Answer, Lord Russell, answer !—King of Heav'n !

" Must Ireland's flocks and herds be always driv'n

" To glut the maw of England? must our corn

" To her huge bursting granaries be borne?   70

" And each hard penny saved from Paddy's rent

" On Indian corn and English ships be spent?

" While year by year the London Rulers count

" So many less in Ireland's gross amount

" Of human beings,—on the other score,   75

" So many thousand sheep and oxen more.

" England has no religion, has no heart ;

" By force and fraud she plays a tyrant part ;

" Fat in the purse, and torpid in the brain,

' Her prayer is pudding, and her God is gain ;   80

" By all mistrusted, and abhorr'd by all ;

" In power unblest—unpitied be her fall !"

Some harken'd well ; but others, growling round,

The voice of Mat in rising murmurs drown'd.

" It's grand, by japers!"—"But the night gets late." 85

" Is it for Coyle and Doran we must wait?"

" I dunno', Barney; *be du hust !* see yonder—

" What can thim two be talkin' of, I wonder."

Captain and Delegate, in muttering speech,

With cool but searching glances, each at each,   90

Stand by the hearth. Big, elderly, and spare,

With serious begging-letter-writer's air,

Some thin locks train'd across his yellow skull,

His features large, yet all the lines are dull,

Small watery eyes, but not a watery nose,   95

Huge fungoid ears, harsh skin befitting those,

O'er many countries has the ' Delegate,'

Through by-paths foul, by unheroic fate

Been hounded ; greedy, discontented, coarse,

Mean, bragging, cringing, full of bad resource ;   100

A man that never could have turn'd to good,

(But might have been to harmlessness subdued)

And to a base perfection rankly grew,

A living lie, a falsehood through and through.

Alone by natural cowardice restrain'd,   105
With blood no less his trembling hands are stain'd,
By murderer, hangman, he in turn has gain'd.
None trusts him less than he with whom he speaks,
That light-built, long-neck'd man with 'brocket' cheeks.
Spoilt priest, attorney's extra clerk, and then   110
Sub-tax-collector, handy with his pen,
But self-conceited, and too sharp of tongue,
Chance after chance Tim Nulty lost, while young,
And now upon a farm (too dear at best),
His brother's transfer when he sail'd out West,   115
Tim poorly keeps a spouse and children five,
And also keeps perpetual war alive
With all above him, caring not the least
For landlord, agent, lawyer, parson, priest ;
Yet talk with Tim, as any stranger might,   120
You'd find him pleasant, lively, shrewd, polite,
With liberal notions, and could scarcely guess
The Ribbon Parish-Master,—Tim's no less.

M

Who next among the various crowd are seen?
That brisk old boy, distiller of *potheen*,   125
A Connaught-man, mellifluous of tongue,
Most plausible of cheating knaves unhung,
Supple, inquisitive, and tough as wire.
Son Jack, a heavy youth in coarse attire,
Begotten by the evil in his sire,   130
Sits next his father, resolute but tame ;
His mode of life adventurous in its frame,
He's still no better than a lumpish clod,
(As doth a mule through alpine passes plod)
Well train'd on moonless nights to watch the still, 135
When light peat-smoke upon the heathery hill
Creeps among rocks and brambles from its cave,
And o'er the dark world, silent as a grave,
The sentry strains his ear for warning shout
Or whistle shrill from valley-guarding scout,   140
Till now the moment long-delay'd bids rush
Their fiery liquor forth in fragrant gush,
Full quickly tasted. All to-night shall taste

The recent venture. Roger cries, "Make haste!"
A perilous ruffian, black-brow'd, strongly built,   145
And through whose face the demon of his guilt
With bulldog's winking eyes of sulky flame
Scowls   at   the   world,   and   knows   not   fear   or
          shame.
His   voice,   like   all   the   man,   is   coarse   and
          rough,—
" Why bluranages, Mattha'! where's the stuff?"— 150
" A lad or two that jined us t'other day,
" We're   waitin'   for."—" Nail   Doran?"—" So   they
          say,"—
" And Dinis Coyle."—To blazes wid the pair!"
—" Doran,"—says one, " consated cub, I'd swear.
—" Larnin!" say others, "What is he to Dan? 155
" And sure he's grandson to a beggarman."
" See   Phil—where   are   you,   Phil?—descinded
          straight,
" Or crooked, from King Flanthach; what consate
" Has Phil at any time? he'll stand a trate

M 2

" All roun' if he has money,—won't you, Phil ? " 160

—" We'll tache them better manners, so we will."

" Dan, whisper, are you bringin' down the jar ? "

" The divil saze them both ! "—" Whisht ! here they

      are."

Sharp-toned his voice, decision on his brow,

With sudden gesture stepping forward now,   165

Their Captain ('Order ! silence !') takes the chair,

And keeps his hat, while other heads are bare.

" All doors well-tiled and truly ?—I declare

" The Lodge is open.   Murty, call the roll.

" I'll punish all defaulters, by my soul !   170

" And now, reports : Young Pat Devanny saw

" Our friend the Scotchman, Alexander Shaw,

" Buying a gun in Lisnamoy last week.

" James Houlahan, the Bear, intends to seek

" For part of Tullagh ; James must get a hint ; 175

" We'll write him on a coffin, in large print.

" Four boys will execute the sentence pass'd

" On Jemmy Burke, convicted at our last

" Of sending in proposals for a farm

" At Meenabo ; they'll do him little harm ;   180

" Dry-beating only, this time. Next fair-day

" Help *from beyond* is coming down our way.

" Burke, with his two brown colts will stand the fair,

" You, Quigly, you, O'Toole, must both be there,

" To keep all day a cat's eye on your man,   185

" And put some whiskey in him if you can.

" You, Doran, that he won't suspect, must draw,

" With two strange lads (they're men you never saw)

" Alongside Jemmy, take him by the hand,

" Call out his name, you know, and make him
         stand,   190

" Until the boys are sure of Mister Burke ;

" Then go your ways for once ; they'll do the work."

Some brethren laugh'd, but all turn'd round to stare

On Doran's face with keen and hideous glare.

" This was submitted and approved. All's right. 195

' You'll get your passwords upon Tuesday night ;

" Next day at three o'clock attend the scout."

Say some, " He hardly likes the job, I doubt."

" Why,   blood   an'   ouns,   Nail   Doran,   you're
            afear'd !"—

" Are you a stagg ?"—and so they scowl'd and jeer'd.

" No stagg !" says fiery Denis ; " on my troth   201

" The word, Jack Farry, ill becomes your mouth."

" Who cares for you ?" Jack Farry quick replies.

" Be done, you blasted fool !" the Captain cries,

" Attention ! silence all !—I now declare   205

" The Lodge is closed.   Be lively Mat, and share,

" The little drop of whiskey ; *glorious news*

" Next night, plase God,—and then we'll have a
            booze."

" What   news,"—" Oul'   Pigot's   wages   will   be
            paid,"—   209

" Ay, troth ! well arn'd, and long enough delay'd."

—" When is it ?" some one whispers. "*Be du
            hust !*

Be du hust, be silent.

" The Grand Heads must approve it, so they must.
—" And what about young Larry ?"—" Soon we'll hear.
" He's well-watch'd in the manetime, niver fear."

The Captain show'd impatience, but the rest   215
Would fain have linger'd o'er the fiery zest.
" Come, Dan, at all evints, a toast, a toast !"
Dan Mullan being as orator their boast ;
A little man with shoulders set awry,
Huge head, flat nose, a grey and furious eye ;   220
Lame in one leg, he limps upon a stick,
Yet few with all their limbs can move so quick ;
Daniel's chief joy is hearing Daniel speak ;
Strong words are his, though utter'd in a squeak ;
And first he flings a fiery glance around,   225
Like chief to warriors on the battle-ground.
" Spake up, Dan !"—" Mount him on a chair !"
       —" Whirroo !"
" Audience for Danel !"

                    " Drink, ye pathriot crew,

" Our frinds in sweet Ameriky an' France !

" To liberáte us may they quick advance,   230

" An' with five hundre' thousan' Paddies bould,

" The Sunburst on their great green flag unrowl'd,

" Sweep every Englishman from say to say

" Into perdition !—O trice glorious day !—

" Immortal cause of Ayrin !—broadsoord, pike,   235

" An' *faugh-a-ballagh*, boys ! we'll nobly strike

" For libertee, for——"

                     So the shrill-voiced Dan,

With furious gestures like a frantic man ;

When lo, the crazy chair whereon he stood

(Which also felt oppress'd, although but wood)   240

Resolving suddenly to bear no more,

Demosthenes lay sprawling on the floor.

His friends approved the soaring words employ'd,

The speaker's downfall they still more enjoy'd,

With shouts of laughter each prolong'd the fun ; 245

But shatter'd lay their glass, their only one.

faugh-a-ballagh, clear the way

A broken teacup soon supplied the want ;
Then oozed the mob away, as drink was scant.
The Delegate, the Captain, and three more,
Remain'd behind : they lock'd and barr'd the door :
Wheels within wheels. The others into night, 251
Some to the merry wakehouse took their flight,
The crowded wake of Rose Muldoon, poor child,
Whose face upon the pillow, pale and mild,
On all her troubles now serenely smiled. 255

   Meantime the secret Five their business do,
And quickly, for the Captain's words are few.
He pulls a scrap of paper from his breast,
And beckons round him, with a nod, the rest,—
" Here is our answer, boys,"—(below his breath) 260
" *Verdict approved on Pigot : sentence Death :*
" Ourselves to fix a proper time and way.
" Our spies, you know, are watchin' every day,
" Moreover, trusty help is close at hand ;
" *The strangers are in town:* you understand. 265

" They only have a certain while to stop ;

" First chance that comes, we'll take it at the hop.

" Meet the Fair-day, my boys, in any case ;

" Pass number twenty—usual hour and place."

  The night before, when Rose was 'taken bad, 270
' The crathur !' off her father ran like mad
For Father Austin.   " Blessed Saints !" they say,
" He'll hardly *overtake her !*—that he may !—
" *Och Wirrastrua !*"—and this awe increased
Moment by moment, till the grave young priest 275
Arriving quickly, set their minds at rest.
Alone with him, the dying girl confess'd
Her slender sins ; then touch'd with sacred oil,
The timid soul from terror to assoyle,
In Bridget's arms her weary head reposed,   280
And Bridget's hands ere long her eyelids closed.
All knew, all cross'd themselves with pious care,
And help'd the parting spirit with a prayer.

                    Wirrastrua ! Mary who art merciful !

The candles soon were lighted for the wake ;
The father saw the tedious morning break,   285
With Bridget, and old women two or three,
Who propp'd their eyelids with perpetual tea.

But *this* night is the great night ; throng enough
In two small rooms, with pipes and plates of snuff,
Laughter and conversation without end.   290
Young Neal, and Denis Coyle his sturdy friend,
Have separate chairs, in token of respect.
Dan Mullan warms upon the sad effect
Of landlords' and their agents' cruel sway
In Rosy's early death,—" Look round, I say !   295
" A white and purty corpse she's lying there,—
" By these five crosses solemnly I swear
" The girl was murther'd !" Reason as you will,
You could not have escap'd the sudden thrill
Which all who heard, and Neal not slightliest felt.
Yet cautiously his cooler judgment dealt,   301

five crosses—made by laying together the fingers of both hands.

While hasty rhetoric in confused debate,

Heap'd on its bulky rubbish, of no weight.

Their own affairs, he saw, they managed ill;

Their chief proficiency, to lie with skill,   305

Ev'n to each other. For this very wake,

To which he gave his mite for Rosy's sake,

Her lazy father, Doran knew full well,

What came to hand would never fairly tell.

" Bloomfield ? who'd ax the tyrant's help ! "—" My
               plan   310

" Would be to take it aff them where we can."

" Whisper !—he ax'd, and got it too."—" How
               much ? "—

" What signifies it ? aisy thing for such,

" Danderin' about the worl' wid pockets full

" O' what they niver arn'd, to sometimes pull   315

" Their han' out."—" True enough ; but don't ye
               think

" Muldoon is boun' to show a drop o' drink ? "

—" Av coorse he is, and that we'll make him do,

"But later in the evenin'—*thigemthu ?* "—

Though Neal and Denis had thought well to come, 320

They never tried to make themselves at home

With this Muldoon, an idle craving sot,

Complaining always of his self-made lot.

View'd from above, the People, widely spread,

Appear a vast and level plain, but tread   325

The lower country, hill and vale are found,

Brooks, thickets, fences, intersect the ground ;

The Many, if with careful eyes you seek,

Among themselves show also class and clique ;

Nor fail'd the friends of Bridget to oppose,   330

At first, her playing nurse's part by Rose.

"I thought so," said the Doctor. "Hum!—I see—

"You gave it, Mr. Bloomfield, on the plea

"Of burial charges ; but it went astray.

"One can't believe a single word they say.   335

"Muldoon had quite enough for proper ends ;

thigemthu, do you understand.

" You made him drunk with all his mourning friends.

" The child was long upon my hands ; and now

" I've plaster'd up the foolish father's brow,

" Who ran his useless head against a wall   340

" When staggering homewards from the funeral.

" Heed him no further ; let him go his gate,

" And reach the workhouse, better soon than late,

" His lawful refuge, and his fitting fate."

The corpse from door of poverty was borne,   345

And yet, of funeral honours not forlorn.

Although Muldoon himself was never sworn,

There march'd *the Lodge*, from greatest man to least,

Her coffin lifted, and would pay the priest.

The heavy bell, which stopt the hearer's breath, 350

At every boom loaded the day with death.

His Curate on his right hand, Priest Adair

Sprinkled the water, said the rapid pray'r.

Clay fell on clay. Some knelt by cross or stone

Before they too departed, leaving lone   355

The ruin'd cloisters, haunted of the wind,

Low-murmuring secrets which no man can find.

Tim Nulty hasted homewards, to compose

A timely burst of dithyrambic prose,

' Another Victim' ; will he sign the letter   360

' Eman-ac-knuck ?' would ' Nemesis ' be better ?—

Proudly shall Tim behold his eloquent rage

Emblazon'd on the *Firebrand's* classic page,

Already fierce on Ballytullagh's woe,

And 'Tiger Pigot' or 'The Poor Man's Foe.'   365

Eman-ac-knuck,' Ned of the Hills, an Irish brigand.

LAURENCE BLOOMFIELD IN IRELAND.

CHAPTER IX.

THE FAIR.

LAURENCE BLOOMFIELD

IN IRELAND.

IX.

THE FAIR.

Ere yet the sun has dried on hedge and furze   1
Their silver veils of dewy gossamers,
Along the winding road to Lisnamoy
The drover trudges and the country boy,
With cows that fain would crop its fringe of sward, 5
And pigs, their hindfoot jerking in a cord,
And bleating sheep; the farmer jogs his way,
Or plies his staff, and legs of woollen gray;
The basket-bearing goodwives slowly move,
White-capp'd, with colour'd kerchief tied above,   10
On foot, or in the cart-front placed on high

To jolt along in lumbering luxury ;
Men, women, pigs, cows, sheep, and horses tend
One way, and to the Harvest Fair they wend ;
Jack Doran with the rest, with sorry cheer,   15
Condemn'd at Pigot's Office to appear,—
To him a place of awe, and doubt, and fear.

  'Tis where the road-side rivulet expands,
And every stone upon its image stands,
The country maidens finish their attire,   20
Screen'd by the network of a tangled briar ;
On grassy bank their shapely limbs indue
With milk-white stocking and the well-black'd shoe,
And court that mirror for a final grace
With dazzling ribbons nodding round their face.   25
Behold our Bridget tripping to the fair ;
Her shawl is splendid, but her feet are bare ;
Till, quick the little bundle here untied,
The shoes come forth, the skirts are shaken wide,
And Biddy enters Lisnamoy in pride ;   30

Nor be it long ere Denis she espies,
To read her triumph in his joyful eyes.

But first of all, with calm submissive face,
Beads in her hand, within the Holy Place
She kneels, among the kneelers who adore   35
In silent reverence on that mystic floor ;
Then with a curtsey, and with symbol meet
On brow and breast, returning to the street.

Crowds push through Lisnamoy, shop, street, and
          lane,
Archway, and yard, corn-store, and butter-crane.   40
Say, as we push, could anywhere be found
A Town more ugly, ev'n on Irish ground ?—
With dwellings meanly low or meanly tall,
With ragged roads, and harsh straight workhouse wall,
With foul decrepit huts, and here and there   45
A roof half-stript and smoky rafters bare ;
With churches that on rival mounts encamp,

One praised for neatness, one admired for pomp;
This, which combines the gaudy and the mean,
(Alas ! the white old chapel on its green)   50
With misplaced ornament that leads your eye
To note the baldness, like a wig awry ;
That, less prodigious, odious not the less,
All prim and trim in tidy ugliness,
A square box with a tall box at the end,   55
While through the wall a stove-pipe's arms extend.
What more ? *these* gates are wide, the passing pray'r
Finds when it will a solemn welcome there ;
Those gates are lock'd, the sexton lets you through,
And shows for sixpence every empty pew ;   60
Here climbs a gilded cross above the roof,
There turns a glittering weathercock aloof ;
Here, every day, the watchful power of Rome,
The English rite on Sundays there at home.
Clean police-barrack perch'd a-top the hill,   65
At foot the dusty slating of a mill,
Townhall betwixt, with many a broken pane,

A squat Wesleyan chapel down a lane,
Make up the total—which, though you despise,
Kindles admiring awe in rustic eyes.   70

Mud hovels fringe the 'Fair-green' of this town,
A spot misnamed, at every season brown,
O'erspread with countless man and beast to-day,
Which bellow, squeak, and shout, bleat, bray, and
         neigh.
The 'jobbers' there, each more or less a rogue,   75
Noisy or smooth, with each his various brogue,
Cool wiry Dublin, Connaught's golden mouth,
Blunt Northern, plaintive sing-song of the South,
Feel cattle's ribs, or jaws of horses try
For truth, since men's are very sure to lie,   80
And shun with parrying blow and practised heed
The rushing horns, the wildly prancing steed.
The moisten'd penny greets with sounding smack
The rugged palm, which smites the greeting back ;
Oaths fly, the bargain like a quarrel burns,   85

And oft the buyer turns, and oft returns;

Now mingle Sassenach and Gaelic tongue;

On either side are slow concessions wrung;

An anxious audience interfere; at last

The sale is closed, and whiskey binds it fast,   90

In cave of quilting upon oziers bent,

With many an ancient patch and breezy rent.

    This afternoon, within the largest tent

Our Bridget sat, with Denis by her side,

A burly boy in youth's full strength and pride;   95

A froth of poetry his ale-cup bore,

For Bridget's sake he fierier draughts forswore;

Love over whiskey joying to prevail,

She sipp'd a cordial, and he quaff'd strong ale.

Her lover's trade was weekly to escort   100

Dead pigs and butter to an eastern port,

To glut the maw of England. "Could we keep

"All food at home, our food would then be cheap,"

Dan Mullan cried in oratoric flow,—

"The very eggs we lay to England go!" 105
But Denis meanwhile profited, and crept
From less to more while patriots groan'd and slept ;
Three busy carts and horses of his own
Along the fifty miles of road were known,
And village after village on the route 110
Heard his loud whip fire off a gay salute ;
Farmer and housewife trusted him to sell,
He sold and traded for himself as well ;
A sturdy generous nature, noway mean,
All saw in him—'tis ever gladly seen. 115
Children love truth, and men, though train'd to lie,
Confess the glowing power of honesty.

Thus let them rest in comfort, happy pair,
While pedlars, tinkers, gamblers, 'work the fair,'
Merchants of apples, cakes, and *spoleen* beef, 120
Most eloquent old-clothesman, silent thief ;
And beggars, thrusting out a blind man's chin,
Or hideous crooked arm or leg, begin,

" In Jesus', Mary's, and Saint Joseph's name,
" Bestow your charitee ! I ax the same   125
" For your dear father's sowl, for your dear mother's,
" If they have parted you—and for your brother's
" And for your sister's sowl ; and that it may
" Appear before the throne o' God this day
" To draw thim out o' Purgathory's flame !   130
" I ax it in the Holy Vargin's name !
" I pray that all your sins may be forgiven !
" And may the comfort and the light of Hiven
" Resave you and your people !"—few would miss
For one poor ha'p'ny such a prayer as this.   135
Murder, and love, and treason, chanted strong
By voices hoarsen'd with perpetual song
Draw each its group ; and ere the rustic buys,
With open mouth to catch the strain he tries,
Then pushing in a rudely bashful fist,   140
Crumples the ill-spelt paper. Who'll enlist ?
Make way ! the Queen's recruiting party come,
Red fluttering flag, assiduous fife and drum,

The haughty sergeant with drawn sword upright,
And two bold swains, their caps with ribbons dight. 145
Now pass the Showmen, with a stronger noise
Of music, and a greater rush of boys,
To mount anew the platform, and invite
Our tardy pence with all their main and might ;
The small boy bangs the loud big drum again, 150
The wheezy pipes renew their shrill refrain,
The shining ladies waltz with wondrous grace,
Loud laughs Tom Fool, and twists his painted face,
Till Irish Damon and his Phillis do
' Walk up ' at last. In turn, well pleased, we view 155
The Peepshow, Nut-gun, Loop, and Fortune's Wheel,
We daff away young chapmen's fly-like zeal,
Whips, pins, bootlaces, crying shrill and loud,
And slowly penetrate th' increasing crowd,
To that worst corner of the noisy Fair 160
In which the furious Tinkers thump and swear.

    Who lays thick cudgel upon ass's hide ?

Who shouting gallops, leg on either side
Grazing the ground? his head behind is shorn,
Thin curls the lean and cunning cheek adorn ;   165
Short coat of frieze, cord breeches to the knee,
A low-crown'd hat, a shirt-neck flying free,
Declare the Tinker, gipsy of our isle,
Tramping with rude black budget many a mile ;
His tribe a partner yields ; his donkey bears   170
At need his children, furniture, and wares ;
Donkeys at many a fair he buys and sells,
And here, among his like, swears loud and yells.
Beyond them are the horses ; there, sweet kine ;
There, flocks of sheep; there, fulsome-smelling swine. 175

   Observe Neal Doran.   Two in pushing past
Give signal due ; the dreadful day runs fast.
He knows the torture now which books reveal ;
Thus, thus it is that malefactors feel ;
Weak, angry, full of fears, condemn'd to know   180
Himself his own inexorable foe.

In front he sees thick tempest, and behind,

The sunny country of· his peace of mind,

As from dark billows a receding shore ;

The simple busy days, now his no more,   185

The perfect slumber in a tranquil bed,

The conscience free of guile and free of dread,

The heart that look'd on every face with love,

The soul that childlike turn'd to God above.

With downcast or unquiet eyes he slinks   190

Among the crowd ; in tent and tavern drinks

Unusual draughts ; then to the Fair-green strides,

Regardless of th' opposing human tides,

To mark the bludgeon's victim, Jemmy Burke,

Most Judas-like : ' the boys will do their work.' 195

The horse-fair Neal is bound for, and his road

Lies through the tinkers, where to shout and goad

The dullest ass his lazy hooves must ply.

'Tis three o'clock ; each noble tinker's eye

Is wet ; the trim shillelaghs wave on high ;   200

Woe to the skull of him who now offends !
In harsh and high-strung temper Doran wends
Amid the tumult ; jostled there, he smites
The intrusive donkey ; fervent word excites
A sharp retort ; all turn to watch the fun ;   205
" Come, hit me !"—'tis no sooner said than done.
Our Youth ('tis all a dream) with rapid blow
And cunning fence, stands foe at face with foe,
Nor, peaceful though his life, unskill'd to wield
The Paddy's wooden pistol, sword, and shield.   210
With planted feet the men are in the lists,
The blackthorns twirl around their nimble wrists,
The meeting weapons play, crick-crack, crick-crack ;
Whilst all push forward, all exclaim 'Stand
          back !'—

More tinkers join ; Neal's partisans pour in ;   215
A wider conflict rages ; fierce the din,
Loud the men's oaths, and sharp the women's
          screams ;
The general fair to this mad whirlpool streams.

At first the tinkers have it all their way ;
Till carman Denis flings apart like spray   220
The clustering mob, and two tremendous blows
Whirls right and left at Neal's two foremost foes ;
On either hand, to earth a tinker goes.
Then shouted Doran's party, pressing on ;
Then shrunk the tinker band, their leaders gone ; 225
Nor had they not been routed, man and ass,
Save for a new event that came to pass.
Lo ! the tall green-coat Guardians of the Law
Wedge through the fight, which feels a sudden awe,
And force away six prisoners to the cells,   230
Deaf to entreaties, protestations, yells,
Regardless of the mob whose stumbling paces
Trot alongside with eager half-turn'd faces.
One tinker's faithful wife pursues their track,
A dirty baby on her dirty back,   235
The bright tin porringers that round her cling
Clashing and flashing gaily as they swing.
She's used to scenes like this ; but not so Neal

And Denis.   What a black disgrace they feel,
In marching thus along the public street !   240
Their misery, for the moment, is complete.

   Since Neal is Pigot's man, the Justice sends
For him ; the brother Justice quick attends ;
Pigot is at his office in the town,
And gladly comes, for reasons of his own.   245
" Receive the tinkers' bail ;—detain these two.
" I'll show you grounds enough for what we do."
—" Your Worship, why keep Denis Coyle and me."
—" Drunk, drunk, you're drunk, sir," says the old J.P.
" Lock, lock them up !" and jerks his bunch of
       seals.   250
They go ; th' untiring rabble at their heels.

   In Pigot's gig came Bloomfield to the fair.
" Evictions please me little, I declare,"
Says Pigot ; " but if men won't pay the rent,
" Or fix conditions, forcing our consent ;   255

" Claiming, when once let in, a better right

" Than ours, for ever, in the law's despite ;

" If still you find to cheat and overreach

" The study, the delight, of all and each ;

" A servile, plausible, and lying brood,   260

" Devoid of honesty, of gratitude ;

" If among people ignorant and misled

" Worse lawlessness begins to grow and spread,

" Till from chicane to murder they aspire,

" And all the foolish mass is catching fire ;   265

" What then ? are we to sit with folded hands,

" And yield ourselves to Captain Rock's commands ?—

" Though Tullagh was a sad affair, I know,

" 'Twill do great good.   Your lands of Meenabo

" Must follow next.   These Dorans, whom you

          praise,   270

" I once thought well of, till I knew their ways.

" I'll show you at the office now (as far

" As may be quickly shown) how these things are ;

" A certain *List* you also shall peruse,

o

" The which I only bide my time to use.   275

" To manage folk like these is hard indeed ;

" 'Tis well for you, sir, that escape the need ! "

Pigot's fast mare by thickening crowds restrain'd

By slow degrees the office-door has gain'd ;

" Room ! " cries the stable-boy, and backward tread 280

Th' obsequious throng, hats fly off every head ;

But ere a tenant's foot may pass the door

The private talk endures an hour or more.

Outside, old Paudheen waits to say his say ;

A short thick man, with sleek head wiry-gray,   285

Projecting underlip, and stunted nose,

Whereon the huge horn-spectacles repose,

When to the service of a writ he swears,

Or ' copy ' with ' original ' compares ;

A sneaking, dauntless man, who disregards   290

Menace or flattery, smoothly plays his cards,

And might perhaps have soar'd, in wider sphere,

Lord Chancellor, Archbishop, or Premier,

But now, victorious in a meaner form,
Has built a nest, and works to line it warm.   295

   'Tis Paudheen carries in the message sent
By brother Justice. Bloomfield's ear is bent
To Pigot's statements ; and he understands
This chiefly—plotting heads and violent hands,
Mad folly, discontentment, fear and hate,   300
In servile seeming, on their footsteps wait.

   In public-house, upon an upper floor,
A thin keen watchful man and some few more
Sit round their drink, but not with laugh or song.
The Parish-Master's summons through the throng 305
Is flitting darkly up and down the street,
And one by one he sees his best men meet ;
The sign said *urgent business.* No delay
A certain case admits of—not one day.
" Let Jemmy Burke go home ; far higher game 310
" Our sportsmen mark,—with license for the same.

" The young bird promised fair and smooth at first ;

" But he can't change things—won't, in case he durst.

" And now the old one's *up*—has all our names,

" The List lies in his pocket. Burning flames   315

" To bed the traitor !—that comes by-and-by."

Glasses were fill'd, refill'd, the quart ran dry ;

Then fist caught fist, and eye shot flame to eye.

" Bail, too, for Coyle and Doran they refuse !

" If we're for action, there's no time to lose.   320

" Well said, my boys ! for though the hazard's great,

" The ball's with Pigot if we hesitate.

" They came to Lisnamoy, but don't go home

" Together ; Minor Bloomfield's horse is come.

" Bill keeps our friend in talk. I understand   325

" Grimes has his noble Honour's gig in hand,—

" Some twist—the patent axle to unscrew—

" A job 'twill take him just an hour to do.

" Tis four at present. To your places, boys !"

The whisper done, they vanish without noise.   330

LAURENCE BLOOMFIELD IN IRELAND.

CHAPTER X.

PIGOT.

LAURENCE BLOOMFIELD
IN IRELAND.

X.

PIGOT.

ALAS, you count me a prosaic bard,
Good reader! Think what Horace says, how hard
It is to sing of every-day affairs.
More willingly by far the minstrel dares
Three flaming dragons than a single pig;   5
Knights in full armour, giants church-tower big,
Are easy folk to handle, by the side
Of one policeman. I have sometimes cried,
' Afford my verse a little touch of aid,
' Thou grave, good-humour'd, venerable Shade,   10
' Who once Comptroller of the Customs wast,
' *Edwardo Rege!*' but my pray'r is lost;

For though our modern telegraph extends
Into that Other World's extremest ends,
Old Chaucer deigns no syllable to say,   15
And I must only do the best I may.

   Bloomfield is also Justice of the Peace,
But has not used his power, but for increase
Of knowledge ; he lets Pigot go alone
To hear this case, its merits not yet known ;   20
And meanwhile in the office musing sits,
Or glancing towards the Ribbon Roll by fits ;
Yet, as it sometimes falls that when we meet
Some wondrous thing, the quest of high conceit,
See, touch, possess, we hardly care to look,   25
To other paths his thought itself betook ;
And still the spy's Black List he chose to hold
As Pigot gave, unloosen'd from its fold.
What he must do, determined,—Bloomfield now
Perplex'd is puzzling over ' when ?' and ' how ?'   30

The careful faces of the tenant throng
Sank with new sense of pity and of wrong
Deep in his heart, their anxious courtesies,
The timid movements of their watchful eyes,
Their air of suffering, which was no pretence,   35
Their piteous lack of manly confidence ;
And most of all, Jack Doran's toilworn face,
Who knows that he has lost his Agent's grace.

Tight has he clung to that poor spot of earth
Which, sixty years since, saw his humble birth.   40
This patch first yielded to his father's spade ;
Those barren hills his life's horizon made ;
To this, a poor, and yet a happy home,
His kindly Maureen, fair young bride, had come ;
Their children here were born, here long reposed   45
His mother's age, and here her eyes were closed.
Content with constant toil and slender gain,
If he and his might there in peace remain,
Old Jack has trudged this morning to the town

To meet bad news ; his heart is sore cast down. 50
Jack had been 'noticed ;' 'twas a usual thing,'
Familiar as a dash of hail in Spring ;
A mode of keeping tenants under thumb :
To-day he hears his fate ; his turn is come.
In short three weeks, Black Paddy tells him so, 55
The Mighty Man has will'd it,—he must go.
In vain the tenant asks to learn his crime,
In vain seeks hope at least of winning time ;
Paudheen is mild, and shakes his cunning pate,
" You'll see himself,"—and sad old Jack must wait 60
In crowded hall, through many weary hours,
His mind, deserted now by half its powers,
Struggling to set itself in some array.
What can he do ? first, what to Pigot say ?
If every other hope and chance should fail,   65
May plea, perhaps, for longer time prevail ?
Not wholly bare, as some do, must he fly,
Yet, seasons have been bad and taxes high,
Wasting away their little store ; let all

Be gather'd, and 'tis pitifully small.   70

Not much has half a century's labour giv'n

This prudent man, who well has watch'd and striv'n,

Industrious, patient, peaceful ; in a land

Less cruel to her sons, his strenuous hand

Had won some better comfort for old age ;   75

The tedious fight he well knew how to wage

With wind and flood, with stubborn rock and clay ;

But selfish men are fiercer foes than they.

Poor useful wrestlers with the rugged soil,

Children of narrow poverty and toil,   80

Who spread the waving plenty o'er the land,

And give the sumptuous palace room to stand,

How much ye do and suffer, to supply

Some easy man with careless luxury !

The wife, the babes, that Heavenly Bounty gave 85

Increase his load of fetters on the slave ;

His sweat absorb'd into a patch of earth,

His life-long labours held of little worth,

Dependent hourly on a rich man's whim,

Whose busy idleness regards not him.   90

No foot of ground, however wild, he owns,

Till in the graveyard rest his weary bones,

Too happy if beside his fathers laid,

Nor coldly cover'd by a poor-law spade.

O Ireland! home of hardship! why do yet   95

Thy children cling to thee? thin cheeks are wet,

Hearts long opprest with care feel poignant woe

As hence from gloom to brighter climes they go.

To each the country of his birth belongs,

Its landscapes, seasons, faces, memories, songs,   100

And he to it; removed to foreign scene,

Though fat in purse, his life is poor and lean;

Forget the past, and flourish as he may,

An exile now, his home is far away.

Shall   Jack   to   Bloomfield   speak?—a   tempting

          thought,   105

Dismiss'd with terror ; what could thus be wrought
But swift destruction of his every hope ?
'Twere dragging tight around his neck the rope ;
High-treasonable conduct, merely mad ;
Training, experience, custom, all forbade.   110
No, the young Landlord neither would, nor could :
—If Jack had only guess'd his Landlord's mood !
So there the Tenant stands disconsolate,
There sits the sturdy Bailiff, big with fate,
Within, the Landlord, thinking ; all await,   115
These and the rest, their Agent's quick return,
With various minds, and faces sad or stern.

But Bloomfield hears a whispering in the hall,
An exclamation, and a sudden fall,—
" 'Tis oul' Jack Doran fainted, 'cause his son   120
" Is taken up on Ribbon business." None
Was quick enough with help when th' old man's brain,
Quite overtroubled, strove no more in vain ;
Anxiety, fatigue, and frugal fast

Had worn him ; then this new blow, and at last 125
From all his limbs the vital vigour fled,
And on the flagstone smote his grey unconscious head.

Strange was the sight before the tenants' eyes :
Young Bloomfield, kneeling on the hall-floor, ties
His handkerchief, a bloodied bandage now,   130
To staunch the wound on old Jack Doran's brow ;
Then to an arm-chair helps him ; soon convey'd
To neighbouring house, where in a bed he's laid ;
While Bloomfield calls to audience Paddy Dhu
In private, which was also something new.   135

When Pigot's eyes met Bloomfield's, instantly
Each felt a moment come, they knew not why.
What's accident ? Aware or unaware,
We to a verge have drawn, reposing there,
Or balanced fine ; until a moment flashes—   140
Down from its level seat firm custom dashes,

Broken, destroy'd,—imprison'd powers escape,

And lo! our life is in a different shape.

" These two young men?"—"Are on that Ribbon
　　　List."

—" Much better proof, a lawyer would insist,　145

" Were needful, ere we clapt them into jail;

" The present charge is trifling, take their bail."

—" Full informations will be laid to-night."

—" So be it—meanwhile, do them legal right."

Pigot, his landmarks of a sudden lost,　150

His mind with novel perturbation tost,

Consented to a message of release;

When more his rage and wonder to increase,

With quiet voice and look, but grave and steady,

Bloomfield spoke thus, and held his papers ready, 155

" All things consider'd, it perhaps were best

" This tenant Doran be not dispossess'd,

" Nor any men of mine, in fact, but three,

" And those are——"

　　　　　　　" Mr. Bloomfield, pardon me,　160

" I cannot be half-agent for your lands.   160

" Unless you leave such business in my hands,

" Allow me to resign the whole to you.

" This I have long, indeed, desired to do."

—" I take your offer."

        Half an hour is flown,

And Pigot in his gig has left the town ;   165

While Bloomfield, with his tenants face to face,

Sees hope and joy, unwonted in that place,

Alive in every look.   They warmly felt

When by the poor old man their landlord knelt ;

'Tis known that Neal and Denis are set free ;   170

And Pigot's gone,—dismissed ?—but that could never

        be !

If Bloomfield were an angel from the skies

They could not hunger more with ears and eyes.

  " I am your Agent and no other man.

" I'll try to do you justice if I can.   175

" Easy for me to live abroad, content

" To see of my estate the half-year's rent ;

" But with the help of Heaven I'll take in hand, 180

" As mine it is by law, this piece of land,

" Think first of men, think second of the soil,

" Discourage lies and sloth, back honest toil,

" The good folk ranged on my side, let me trust,

" At war with knaves and fools, if so we must. 185

" If threat'ning letters fly as thick as snow,

" If murderers dog me every step I go,

" They shall not turn me from a settled course,—

" Unless I fall, and then you may have worse.

" Here are the names, within this folded sheet, 190

" Of Ribbon Lodge Two-Sixty, all complete.

" I have not redd it—I'm not fond of spies—

" Now ! see it burn : in ashes there it lies.

" *This* paper is my list of tenants' names,

" Their families, their holdings, debts, and claims. 195

" Slowly we must proceed ; but with good will

" We may, perhaps, together climb the hill."

P

Pigot of late, in health or soul deprest,
Had felt a frequent wish for change or rest
As pictured by his wife, but would not yield   200
To her, still vanquish'd in discussion's field.
He will not own what sometimes he suspects,—
" 'Tis but my wife's timidity infects.
" Hard work these hyppish fogs will soon dispel ;
" I know my business, and I do it well.   205
" Let others please their fancy and their taste,
" Let others fling their idle days to waste,—
" This is no more than fog, by sleep or dinner
          chased."

Yet sometimes, in his own despite, began
The shrewd, experienced, unromantic man,   210
Since now the newness of success was fled,
And years were numbering thickly on his head,
And sense of power had lost its pungency,
To say, what profits it ? what comes to me ?
What is indeed accomplish'd by my life ?   215
The fears and sad forebodings of his wife,

Renew'd by every tale of peasant crime,

Struck heavier on his spirit time by time :

" Throw off this yoke—we've money and to spare,

" Come, let us travel, pitch our tent elsewhere, 220

" And for our children and ourselves enjoy

" A wider world, a life without annoy."

Still, Pigot knows, though discontentment lurk,

He's most at ease in his habitual work,

Within his line, courageous, strong, and tall, 225

Beyond it, even timid, weak, and small ;

His narrow education, flowerless mind,

By no artistic faculty refined,

Are then exposed, himself can partly see.

Like ancient groom or stableman is he, 230

At home on horseback, spite of prance and bound,

A waddling cripple, place him on the ground.

And now—a vile vexation, bitter sting !—

He, both of landlords and of tenants King,

Intending by-and-by to abdicate, 235

With fitting dignity, his power and state,

For private wealth and ease—O sudden shame!

Dismiss'd by one he thought so mild and tame;

Dismiss'd, discharged, ejected as it were

On shortest notice—this was hard to bear.   240

Himself, no doubt, had in a moment's heat

Flung out the startling hint, but self-conceit

Expected never such response to meet.

Long years he has been shaping to his mind

The Harvey-Bloomfield properties combined :   245

Now all his plans are snapt, with bitter sense

Of broken power—of standing on defence.

True, the Young Man, with cautious words and
            kind,

Which well announced a gravely settled mind,

Left to his easy choice the time and mode :   250

But, all things alter'd, and with guard and goad

Tormenting him, can Pigot trace the threads

Of that intricate web that round him spreads,

And disengage it smoothly? well aware,

Amid his mind's perturbed and formless care,   255
Of many questions asking quick replies,
Of many dubious doings that arise
From dusty corners where they lay forgot.
Small days of judgment bring forth many a blot.

Yet here too came experience to his aid,   260
And whisper'd, this confusion once allay'd,
To-morrow's light a clearer path will show,
And all go well enough, as such things go.
" Come up, old mare ! " with cheery voice he cried ;
And Doyle the under-bailiff, by his side,   265
At Pigot's moody silence wondering much,
Felt comforted ; as, to the light-thrown touch
Of whip and voice, the bay mare quickly stept,
And from the high-road to the bye-road swept.

Pigot had seen his fine new house arise,   270
With promise of an earthly paradise,
Amidst a broad, well-cultivated plain,

Trimm'd off with new plantation, fence, and drain ;
Window and door in city-villa taste,

With stucco-ornaments and columns graced,   275
Square spacious rooms, fill'd full of splendid things,
Bright rosewood tables, gilded curtain-rings ;
But, ten years old, the place shines rawly still,
Th' instinctive touch of strong yet tender skill
Quite absent, which we name artistic sense ;   280
Glaring the want, for glaring the pretence ;
Harsh lights upon discordant colours fall,
Large, costly, dull engravings deck the wall ;
Chair, ottoman, by some unlucky doom,
Door, window, fire, stand wrong in every room ; 285
Lawn, green-house, garden, wear no magic beauty,
Shrub, flower-bed, border, stand as though on duty ;
Best thing the farm-yard, practical and neat,
With swine, calves, poultry, stacks of hay and wheat ;
With huge farm horses, and sleek, patient cows, 290
Byres, sheds, and new machines, carts, tools, and
         ploughs.

See at the window Mrs. Pigot stand,

The latest empty novel in her hand ;

A fading woman, but she once was fair,

Whose wealth and pride have many a thorn of care ; 295

A full-dress visit to receive or pay,

Her chief engrossment,—'tis a chalk-white day

That gives a chance to study well the style

Of Lady Harvey's toilette, tone, and smile.

Her servants plague her ; and her children vex, 300

Tearing their clothes, imperilling their necks.

On shaggy Sheltie in and out through trees

Flits Percy at full gallop ; now she sees

Bold Jem and little Ulick at the pond

Sailing forbidden ships ; then looks beyond,   305

With sigh at such perversities, to catch

(Behind the time a full hour by her watch)

The coming gig. Her husband's jolly face,

Fond of his Bess, his children, and his place,

Good-humoured and indulgent for the most,   310

Nor tender pleasure from his glances lost,

Still makes for her the sweetness of her life;
In short, he is her husband, she his wife;
Whatever teasing troubles they endure,
The gentle bond is always firm and sure.   315

  To Newbridge House the pretty bye-way goes,
'Tween scarlet-berried hawthorn and wild rose,
Rowan and woodbine ; the dark-fruited briar
Bends to its bordering grass, through which aspire
The yellow hawk-weed and blue scabious-ball;   320
Grass full of grasshoppers, and flies, and small
Innumerable things. You sometimes hear
A distant voice, or warbling near and clear
Poor-Robin's plaintive melody, at one
With the mild glory of the sinking sun,   325
Which now, completing this autumnal day,
Looks from the great world's end with parting
          ray,
O'er all the golden landscape with its sheaves,
And through the curtain of the wayside leaves.

Across the road a new-cut holly lay.   330
Doyle must alight to drag it from their way.
Through Pigot's heart and brain a sudden gush
Whirl'd all his life to fever : mad thoughts rush
Around their burning prison : " I am caught !"—
And hasty fingers his revolver sought.   335
One terrible moment—courage all drawn dry
To earthquake-ebb—and ere the wave pour high
Returning, from the hedge beside him broke
Two sharp explosions, two white puffs of smoke ;
The mare leap'd round, and gallop'd off pell-mell, 340
But heavily to earth her master fell.

No longer Mrs. Pigot bears to wait ;
She sends a horseman by the lower gate ;
Who rides not far. A man came running fast ;
'Twas bailiff Doyle, pale, breathless, all aghast ; 345
" He's shot ! they've kill'd him !"—and the servants
          found,
Three furlongs distant, prostrate on the ground

Amidst a pool of blood, James Pigot's form,
A dreadful burden, lifeless, though still warm.

   James Pigot's race is run : and shall we call   350
This man a victim, or a criminal ?
Or one who with men's natures coarsely dealt,
Drew out their evil, and its fury felt ?
He did so ; but not his alone the blame.
Elsewhere he might in peace have lived the
      same,   355
And breathed away at last a quiet breath,
No worse than most men in his life and death.
But where the subtle powers of Circumstance,
Multiplex operations that advance
Out of the boundless Bygone World, and make   360
The Present with the flitting forms they take,
Are in an evil seethe like wizard's pot,
Who stirs the same, 'tis now and then his lot
To catch the spurted venom. Where one dies,
Hundreds escape ; and danger ever tries   365

To wear a mask of innocence ; no less,
They cook and finger a strong poison-mess.

Fair-evening as it was, no friendly hand
Lifted the dead ; the people chose to stand
Far-off, or take the fields, or else turn back,   370
But not to follow on the murderers' track ;
Not one made haste to give policemen word ;
By special message first the news was heard.

For many weeks from every wall and gate
Stared 'MURDER' and 'REWARD' in letters great, 375
Two Hundred Pounds the Lord Lieutenant's bribe,
One Thousand which the gentry round subscribe,
But all in vain ; for, his employer dead,
The Spy took mortal fear to heart, and fled.
Few even dared to read the bills, and they   380
Walk'd off in silence ; if they said their say,
'Twas said with caution and in secrecy.
A huge converging crowd of low and high

Had swell'd the costly funeral, and flow'd
In solemn pomp, outstretch'd along the road.   385
The native press was vocal, and the *Times*
Anew said something old on Irish crimes.

And meanwhile, bringing softly night and day,
The round Earth roll'd on her appointed way,
With dead and living, 'mid the starry quire;   390
Brimm'd with material and celestial fire,
And to and fro, with emmets' briskness, ran
The shifting, multifarious brood of Man.

LAURENCE BLOOMFIELD IN IRELAND.

CHAPTER XI.

LORD AND LADY.

LAURENCE BLOOMFIELD
IN IRELAND.

XI.

LORD AND LADY.

Virgil, Tom Tusser after him, have sung
The rules of farming with melodious tongue ;
And shall my Muse make venture ? not afraid,
If need there were, to call a spade a spade.
Too oft, neglecting fashion, she incurs   5
The public's coldness and the publisher's ;
Yet now she will not rival Martin Doyle
On farms, and drains, on light and heavy soil,
Clod-crushing, ploughing, and rotation meet
Of grass, potatoes, barley, turnips, wheat,   10
Ovine and bovine breeds—

                             Thou youngest Grace !

Dear Maiden of the shy and eager face
In drooping darkness framed, or ripply gold,
And spirit like the fresh bud half unroll'd
To morning's light !—O Boy of many dreams,   15
Through sacred woods and by enchanted streams
Far wandering forth in reverie divine !—
Ye cannot love such dismal verse as mine.
Sweet friends, forgive me ! I have sung for you
Erewhile, if but a little song or two ;   20
For you I dearly hope to sing again ;
Though now, perhaps, with labour all in vain,
Striving to melt and mould of stubborn stuff
(It could be rounded, were there fire enough)
A living shape harmonious, part and whole   25
Completed fitly by th' informing soul.

And yet I will not rival Martin Doyle,
Mechi, or Stephens ; 'twere a thankless toil.
For, every rule and detail strictly given
Whereby our Laurence in his course has thriven, 30

(With labour, and with stumbling, and mistake,
And disappointments and defeats, that break
The fragile purpose, but confirm the strong)
Another man were scarcely help'd along,
Who deals with different people, different facts.   35
Mere sons of action, piecing up their acts
Of work and life, incalculable deem
The soul, or quite omit it from their scheme,
Or, like Napoleon, use it, while they scorn :
A miracle as true as birth of morn,   40
As simple as the imperial sun's broad light
Bathing earth's planet ; with as vast a might
It works in silence on the spaces vast
And crowds of things within its influence cast.

  Bloomfield had plunged, as though into the sea ; 45
But soon recover'd equanimity
Amidst the new demands and powers unknown,
Nor any force to help him save his own.
Confused, and dim, and dangerous appear'd

Q

His enterprise, but soon the prospect clear'd : 50
Most men can do as much for duty, gain,
Opinion, pleasure ; call it a campaign
At worst, but that's too serious ; travel brings
More toil and risk ; or fifty other things.
Arithmetic's plain rules his purse shall guard, 55
And every lesser luxury he'll discard
Till this of playing king be fairly tried.
Of Indolence, for ever at our side,
Subtlest of demons, Laurence knew full well
The sleepy goblet, drugg'd and dregg'd with hell, 60
And hung upon his neck the counterspell
Of daily work sufficient for his force,
And so set bravely forward on his course,
With much to hinder, but with nought to stay,
Finding undreamt-of help along the way. 65
For still to him who on himself depends
The lumbering, veering world its succour lends ;
The bold are help'd by poison, storm, and fire,
Against the weak, flow'rbuds and lambs conspire.

Thus, when young Bloomfield had survey'd his ground,

He certain chances in his favour found.

No legal right existed but his own,

He was the State, like Lewis, he alone,

Or rather raised to an autocracy

Temper'd with murder, as in Muscovy ; 75

There, sole, stood he, there lay his subject lands,

To do, or not do, resting in his hands.

Moreover, if the Celt be rash and wild,

Quick, changeful, and impulsive, like a child,

He looks with somewhat of a childlike trust 80

To those above him, if they're kind and just ;

Be tender to his moods, allow a whim,

No surly independence lurks in him ;

Content with little, easy to persuade,

The man who knows him speaks and is obey'd. 85

If sprung from history, circumstance, or race,

Or all together, Bloomfield well could trace,

With aid from childhood's memory, manhood's

thought—

And into every plan his knowledge wrought—
A special Irish character. With those   90
Of higher station, harder to oppose,
His even temper, frank and courteous speech,
And true unselfishness, with all and each,
His firmness and concession, sped him well;
His sense and knowledge soon began to tell;
Till all who dealt with public plans descried
The need to weigh him, on whatever side.

  To men and books an open ear he lent,
He studied silent Nature much, and went
With careful tireless footstep after hers;   100
The cheer which knowledge flowing in confers
Was his, and then the artist's joy, to find
The rugged world take pressure from his mind.
His rental, even, to his own surprise,
Reach'd its old mark, and then began to rise; 105
A sort of proof he could have done without,
Yet good firm hold against the twitch of doubt.

Look round from Croghan Lodge, and not in vain
You seek the records of a seven years' reign ;
So long have Laurence and his Queen borne rule. 110
The smoky hovel with its fetid pool
Has disappear'd—poor Paddy's castle-moat,
Which kept the foulness, let the use run out ;
White walls, gay rustic gardens meet your eyes,
Trim gates and fences, haggarts, barns and styes ; 115
Down the wet slope a net of drainage spreads ;
The level marsh waves wide with ozier-beds ;
Among the barren folds of windy hills,
Round solitary loughs, by rock-strewn rills,
And up to crags that crown the heathery steep, 120
Larch, pine, and sycamore begin to creep ;
Old bog and scraggy moorland, parcell'd out,
Have busy hands at work,—no fear or doubt
To dry up half their strength, for Bloomfield chose
The likeliest people, lent waste ground to those, 125
" The first year so much done—so much in five—
" Push onwards, win the battle, you shall thrive

" Rent-free so long—so long at little rent—
" And then a lease that makes us both content."
New roads run round the hills, and to the shore ; 130
By-lanes engulf the hapless wheel no more ;
While certain paths defended tooth and nail
By Pigot, often sending men to jail,
Without another word of wrong or right
Lie free as air is to the swallow's flight.   135

Broad open too lies Bloomfield's own domain,
Park, fields, and wood, from mountain-top to plain ;
The lough's green isles in wavy silver set ;
The cool crypts of the rocky rivulet.
Sunk fence, light paling, leave the prospect free ; 140
Fair run the road and path, by sward and tree ;
No churlish prison-wall defeats your eye,
Robs of the landscape every passer-by,
Shuts up the great horizon in a box,
Boon Nature's beauty in a harem locks   145
For one rich Turk ; no board devoid of shame

Tickets the world with one poor selfish claim ;

For no proud porter must you ring and wait ;

The stile is low, and easy swings the gate ;

The devious wood-walk, far-commanding hill,   150

The ferny dingle, these are yours at will ;

Or in that high fir-temple would you be,

Which makes perpetual music like the sea,

And on the sunset lifts its pillars black ?

Across the lough, across the plain look back.   155

Look back : no single cottage-roof is there

In Bloomfield's charge, that knows not Bloomfield's
    care.

In spots the best for landscape or for shade

You find the solid rustic-benches laid ;

And on the highroads, also, weary feet   160

Approach with grateful haste the new stone seat,

Here, nigh a well, or there, with slanting shed

To guard from rain or sun the traveller's head.

 In Croghan Hall, when new, the famous Dean,

Upon his journeys, moody guest hath been.   165
Well-built at first, but mouldy with neglect,
Young Laurence as his own chief architect
Chose out the shrewdest workmen that he might,
And made the mansion safe and weather-tight,
Improving all, yet zealous to retain   170
Each stone and tile, each form, each weather-stain.
His own true touch alive on every part
Gave without cost the luxury of Art,
Which foolish Wealth on ostentation set
Can dearly pay for, but can rarely get.   175
'Tween lough and mountain, grove on either hand,
A solid, stately House you see it stand,
Of broad, low stairs, and windows deep recess'd ;
In front, a boundless prospect to the west,
In rear, a terraced garden.   Order reigns,   180
But not with costly and elaborate pains,
A disproportion of the means and end,
Whereby so often wealthy homes offend,—
With vile adornment oft offending worse,

Slapping across our teeth a heavy purse.   185
Good sense, refinement, naïvety, reconcile
Man's work and nature's, and the genial smile
Is brotherhood's, not condescension's, here ;
No bitterness flows in, but strength and cheer
From every aspect ; 'tis a kindly place,   190
That does not seem to taunt you with its grace,
But, somehow, makes you happy, stray or stay,
And pleased to recollect it when away ;
For manners thus extend to house and field,
And subtle comfort or discomfort yield.   195

   Enter : you find throughout the spacious rooms,
If bright, or mellow'd with delicious glooms,
Instead of gaudy paper, silk, and paint,
Statues and pictures, books, wood-carvings quaint,
Dim-splendid needlework of Hindostan,   200
Grave solid furniture of useful plan ;
Here a soft blaze of flow'rs in full daylight,
There, ivied casement, shadowing aright

The mournful relics of the secret Past,
Waifs, liftings, from that ocean deep and vast,   205
The thought and work of many a vanish'd race;
The life of ancient Erin you may trace
In Druid's torque, moon-shaped, of thinnest gold,
Square bell that to St. Patrick's preaching toll'd,
Cups, coins, and fibulæ, and ogham-stones,   210
Spear, axe, and arrow-heads, of flint or bronze.
Whatever knowledge (at the best but small)
Of such is extant, Laurence knows it all,
And sometimes to his neighbours far and near
Imparts a modest lecture, short and clear,   215
On things Hibernian, chiefly those around,
The Giant's Grave, the Fort, the Fairy-Mound,
The crumbling Abbey-wall, the Round-Tower grey,
Still rising smooth and firm as on the day
Its taper cap received the topmost stone;   220
The mountain Cairn, to distant counties shown;
The Norman-English Keep on river brink;
His light firm hand connecting link with link

Of Irish history, so that none complain
To find it gall them like a rusty chain.   225
This large room is for music ; violin,
Piano, voice, at times the merry din
Of Bloomfield's rustic band, its echoes wake,
And rustic hearers oft an audience make.

Nay, all with ears to hear, with eyes to see,   230
To every sight and sound have welcome free.
To make our costly luxuries right and fair
All human beings who are fit must share.
So Bloomfield said, was laugh'd at, yet he tried,
Found all come easy, nor the rule too wide.   235

But haste we !—'Tis that merry time of year,
Once more brought round upon our whirling sphere,
(The days of darkness and of snow gone past,
Of chilly sunbeams and the freezing blast),
When eager skylarks at the gate of morn   240
Keep singing to the sower of the corn

In his brown field below; the noisy rooks
Hold council in the grove-top; shelter'd nooks
Bring forth young primroses and violets;
The woodland swarms with buds, the ash-tree sets 245
Dark lace upon his bough,—with tenderest green
The larch-spray tufted, pallid leaflets seen
Unfolding and uncrumpling day by day.
Nigh Croghan Hall the herons lean and grey
Hover and float upon those wide-spread wings   250
Around their lofty cradles, with the Spring's
Breath rocking slowly; braird is pushing through;
The clever mavis and the soft cuckoo
Untiring sing their olden songs anew;
In fields of freshest grass the bold young lambs 255
Jump lightly round their anxious bleating dams;
And little Mary Bloomfield, blithe as they,
Greeting a happy morn of holiday,
The sunshine glittering on her golden head,
Runs races through the lawn with brother Fred 260
("He's but a child," says Mary; he is four,

His comrade and protectress two years more,)

Among the clumps of yellow daffodils.

Light blows the breeze, a vernal freshness fills

The morning sky, green plain, and dappled hills, 265

As run the merry babes with floating hair,

Watch'd by their parents. After morning pray'r

And breakfast, and while busy hands complete

A children's banquet-hall with flow'r and sweet,—

" What say you, Jenny, young folk, shall we drive? 270

" 'Tis four long hours before our guests arrive."

Smoothly the simple carriage speeds along

Behind two chestnut ponies brisk and strong,

By Laurence guided : he looks older now,

But bears his candid, smooth, and open brow 275

Uncreased with petty cares, fine mouth unseam'd

With policy ; the ripening years have spread

His tall and goodly frame ; free lifts his head

Its brownish clusters. By him sits Queen Jane.

No queen ?—look closer—she deserves to reign. 280

How is she drest? Madam, in shawl cream-white,

Straw bonnet, trimmed with purple, if I'm right.

She is not tall, and rather dark than fair,

Her forehead fitted close with soft black hair,

Brows sloped the right way, over eyes so true,   285

Eyes darkly clear, I cannot tell their hue,

That faith and courage kindle where they gaze,

Earth is not vulgar, lighted with those rays ;

Fine ear, a nostril flexible and thin,

Lips mildly proud, a full but gentle chin,   290

Compact and firmly-moulded foot and hand,

Gesture and look accustom'd to command,

Or rather to be willingly obey'd

As having never o'er the boundary stray'd

Of others' rights and feelings,—such is she ;   295

A trustier human creature cannot be ;

Mild, gracious, and undaunted, every line

Of soul and body nobly feminine.

Instinctive wisdom, humour swift and gay,

A simple greatness, sure to do and say   300

The best, belong to her, and in her voice

A tone to make the dullest heart rejoice.
No marvel if the servants of her home
Are humble friends, if cordial blessings come
To every peasant's lip that forms her name,   305
If my poor stumbling pen forebears for shame.
O happy Husband!—happy Wife no less!
In perfect mutual trust and tenderness,
Whatever joys await the Blest above,
No boon below like happy wedded love.   310

Down the park-slope, Lough Braccan full in view,
Boss'd with green islands floating on the blue,
Through well-kept farms, by neat white cottages,
Boglands reclaimed, new belts of rising trees,
Paddock and croft, with many a feather'd brood, 315
Lambs, calves and foals, (life everywhere renew'd)
That send their voices on the lightsome air,
And of the vernal day enjoy their share,
Gay speed we. That's the steward's house,—his name
Neal Doran (he's the same, and not the same); 320

His wife and he are up at Croghan Hall,

Best aids to trim our little festival.

There's Lisnamoy church-spire, and further down

The Romish steeple ; midway in the town

Stands up the clock-tow'r, whose melodious tongue 325

Calls noon, a civic voice to old and young

To draw them in a circle, voice of Time

To each and all—O hearken ! says the chime :

Reckless, who will now and then respect

That preaching, if all others they neglect.   330

There, to new Market-place a pipe conveys

A cold perpetual water-vein, which plays

All day and night with cheerful soothing tone,

Falling into its shallow tank of stone

In curving crystal fringed with showery spray ;   335

Where sometimes, doubtless, girls and dames delay

With rested pitchers, till a warning stroke

Cuts short at last the gossip and the joke.

Carved shamrocks, mixt with field-flow'rs, grass, and

corn,

The stone rim of the dial-face adorn ; 340

Atop, a sleeping infant, left and right

Stout peasant-man and woman, holding tight

A sickle and a basket ; rudely true,

The sculpture to a rustic hand is due

And Bloomfield's brain, who, whilst his neighbours

       smiled, 345

With jutting balcony and roof red-tiled,

Built his Town-hall at less than half the cost

(The which in sooth impress'd his neighbours most)

Of Pigot's plan, in classic British taste,

With sequences of scroll and bracket graced. 350

Each year the town receives improvements, plann'd

By no expensive, by no vulgar hand ;

New house with window'd gable to the street,

Ruin displaced, and ragged wall made neat,

Good drains, and whitewash, footwalks, and young trees ;

The change in Lisnamoy each traveller sees, 356

And almost sings aloud with joy to win

' The Bloomfield Arms,' a clean and cosy inn,

R

Where Denis Coyle and Bridget welcome you;
Not as the dismal 'Royal' wont to do,   360
With shabby waiter, old and drunk, proud host
And sluttish chambermaid, poor fare, high cost.

We drive through Lisnamoy.   Who bows so low?
Father Adair : but well does Bloomfield know
Of Bloomfield's favourite School the deepest foe. 365
There stands the building, comely brick and stone,
A little backward from the causeway thrown,
Flower-beds and paths in orderly array,
And greensward for the noon's half-hour of play ;
All empty now, for eldest child and least   370
Must share at Croghan Hall the Vernal Feast.
The School has prosper'd, and is prospering still,
Though absent every clergyman's good-will,
Who each would make a primer of his creed,
Since now the vulgar must be taught to read,   375
The bigot duly with the scholar train,
Weed out man's brotherhood from breast and brain,

Twist every thought and feeling as they grow,—
Neighbour baptized to live his neighbour's foe.
Rome's churchmen seized the new scholastic dower,
Secure to swell by just so much their power,   381
While haughty shepherds of the legal rite
Declared this vulgar partnership a slight,
And loud demanding separate purse and place,
Flung a big Bible in the statesman's face,   385
Who handed back the volume with a bow.
So wrath was kindled, and is burning now,
In minds too Christian or perhaps too proud
To fill the legal hour for them allow'd,
Since Popish pastors that same right enjoy'd   390
With their own lambs, nor left it unemploy'd.
But now the people's alphabet in turn
Must from its first supporters feel the spurn.
How, for one day, could we, shrewd Men of Rome,
Forget th' experience, now again brought home,   395
That Knowledge acts as poison, if 'tis not
Cook'd in the black ecclesiastic pot,

From cardinals' and bishops' high discourse
Down to the *a b c* of babes at nurse ?
As Spain puts garlic into every mess,   400
So must the sacred flavour more or less
Be mix'd in every atom of the food,
To dye the bones and circle with the blood ;
Arithmetic the one true Church must own,
And Grammar have its orthodoxy known ;   405
Or else, keep free from learning's dangerous leaven,
Guided, in blessed ignorance, to Heaven.
But well the People know how great the boon :
We must not drive, but lead and coax them : soon,
Whene'er the wind political turns fair,   410
Help'd by our foes, who also seek their share,
We pull the pagan system down perforce,
Its wealth and strength made chiefly ours, of course.
Meanwhile, wherever possible, let schools
In strict accordance with our holy rules,   415
With every fitting gesture, form, and phrase,
Supplant these others, yet no war-cry raise.

Pigot, who did but little know or care,
Was wrought upon by Father John Adair,
Slighted the 'National,' and had almost   420
(For keeping with the clergy was his boast)
Promised the 'Christian Brotherhood' a site.
But Bloomfield came, and alter'd things outright,
Obtain'd a Model School for Lisnamoy,
Built other schools, and saw that girl and boy   425
Who might go, did go, for he knew his ground,
And soon the People in his party found ;
Whereon Adair, the smooth and patient man,
Howe'er he felt, lock'd up his favourite plan,
And neither bann'd nor bless'd the Model School,
Paying due visits, as by legal rule.   431
The parish was improved, his income raised ;
He oft (perhaps sincerely) Bloomfield praised.

Inn, fountain, clock, we pass, and quit the town
Close by the Workhouse, where with Isaac Brown 435
Hath Bloomfield many a tedious battle fought,

And many a good reform full slowly wrought ;
For weekly there, sat once a Guardian Board
To guard the landlords' purse from pauper horde,
To guard the bed where age and sickness lie   440
From touch of comfort—let them live or die,—
What matter how their drop of life runs by ?
To guard poor children, trembling little slaves,
Cast on our pity by misfortune's waves,
From spade and needle, watching lest they learn 445
The skill that might a scantest living earn,
Using, faith, hope and charity being dead,
Political-economy instead,
Training with anxious negligence a race
To live their country's burden and disgrace.   450
Sad without guilt, and punish'd without crime,
Those joyless children dragg'd their weary time,
Or issuing from their prison two by two
Distress'd the road with cheeks of ghastly hue,—
Unlike the brisk though tatter'd urchins there,   455
Not highly fed, but free from Guardians' care.

Now much is alter'd : it were long to tell,

But now both young and old are nourish'd well,

The Master's not a drunkard or a fool,

No roguish dunce pretends to teach the school,   460

Each boy or girl receives an honest trade,

And starts in life with small sufficient aid.

Nor is it found to swell the pauper list :

The Board on steady discipline insist,

Make all those work who can, and seldom fail   465

Where punishment is due. 'Tis worse than jail

For all the bad and lazy ; but the child,

The sick, the hoary head, meet liberal hand and mild.

Next the neat Vicarage gate we swiftly reach,

Where Reverend Mr. Jones's little speech   470

Upon the weather gives a moment's pause,

Deliver'd sweetly with due hems and haws.

The gout one day despatch'd old Vicar Boyd ;

Whereon—since craft had vainly been employ'd

To draw from Laurence Bloomfield what he meant,

For he, lay-rector, could his choice ' present,'   476
And two far cousins of the reverend class,
And ten times more their lady wives, alas !
Had loathed each other on this ground for years—
Behold an aguish time of hopes and fears.   480
" What *will* you do, then ?"   " Nothing ! "—with a
      smile.
" I leave it with the Bishop."   (Is this guile,
Or idiot folly, or unfeeling jest ?)
" With him, entirely,—Bishop must know best."
His Lordship sent a parson mild and tame,   485
Glad of the glebe ; and when his Lordship came
On confirmation tour, with whom was he
So cordial as with Bloomfield, or so free ?
At Croghan Hall, too, did the great man dine,
And made himself delightful o'er the wine.   490

  But now for home.   Our merry wheels forsake
Close hedgerows for the margin of the lake,
Edged with these water-gnawn fantastic stones

That show its winter level, white as bones.
The unimprison'd eye skims, miles on miles,   495
The silver distance, and the verdurous isles
That slumber on their shadows in the smooth,
And back to where fine lipping ripples soothe
Its nearer beach. High snort the ponies proud,
Fish leap, young Fred and Mary laugh aloud   500
For very joy of life. We quit the shore,
Wind up the hill, and halt at Croghan door.

At two all's ready. Gathering, trooping fast,
Bright happy faces, all are here at last ;
Clad, boy and girl, blue, red or duffel-grey,   505
In homespun garments most, a trim array.
Their entertainers greet them, recognise
One here, one there : now break we, and devise
All merry games among the grass and trees,   509
'Tig,' ' Hide & Seek,' ' High Windows,'—what we please ;
Till, like a bee-drum, sounds the welcome call
To tea and dainties in the music-hall ;

Nor music silent, of the rustic band ;
Laurence and Jane with friendliest eye and hand
To each in turn attentive. Banquet done,   515
Forth draws them once again the westering sun,
Some dancing in the many-circled mound,
Thick with primroses, others seated round ;
And there they sing in chorus, till the light
At last begins to fade. Lo ! rushing bright,   520
A culminating rocket bursts aloft
In gold and crimson meteors, drooping soft ;
Another follows ; wondrous wheel and gyre
Spin on the grovy background shapes of fire ;
A blue ecstatic splendour, mildly strong,   525
Bathes tree and mansion, mound and gazing throng;
Then dusk, as of a sudden, wraps the scene,—
All memory now ; remembered well, I ween.
In careful cart and wagon home are sent
The smaller children, sleepily content ;   530
The rest, drawn up in order at the door,
March with their trusty Captains as before.

" All children can be govern'd : with the best

" Much may be done; and something with the rest.

" Of men, to help you or be help'd, choose first 535

" The best you know of; and avoid the worst :"

Thus Bloomfield,—though, like Dunstan, he could dare

To pinch the Devil's nose, if need there were.

He found, being active yet averse from strife,

'Twas not so hard to live a manly life ; 540

Or call it godly life, and thereto read

The learn'd and holy necromantic Swede ;

Wildest and wisest of the dreamers he.

All dream, but foolish visions most men see.

LAURENCE BLOOMFIELD IN IRELAND.

CHAPTER XII.

M I D S U M M E R.

LAURENCE BLOOMFIELD

IN IRELAND.

XII.

MIDSUMMER.

Now early sink away the starry Twins,

Pursuing sunset ; eastern heaven begins

To lift Arcturus, with that Coronet

Upon the brow of Summer glittering set ;

And rich the country now, with shady roads

And hollow lanes embank'd with fern ; white *loads*

Of fragrant hawthorn-bloom, but when this bloom

Grows fainter, bramble-roses in its room ;

And sunny paths for milkmaids, winding through

The grass thick-set with yellow flow'rs and blue, 10

Millions of little blue and yellow flow'rs ;

Rich are the warm, long, lustrous, golden hours,

That nourish the green javelins of the wheat,
The delicate flax, the tufted clover sweet,
And barley's drooping beard, and speckled oats.　15
The yorlin's trembling sigh of pleasure floats
On sultry wind ; the landrail's hoarse crake-crake
Still keeps the meadows and cornfields awake
When two clear twilights mingle in the sky
Of glowing June.

　　　　　　　A broad white margin dry　　20
Around Lough Braccan, yet our four-oar'd boat
At this long jetty's end lies well afloat.
Your hand, fair London girl ; your hand, my Jane ;
Lord Camlin lifts wee Molly ; Fred is fain
Of Pictor's hand, the glowing P. R. B.　　25
Two elder guests embark more leisurely,
Grave William Downing, an official man,
George Roe, as grave, but on a different plan,
Our Irish antiquary,—both exact,
Elaborate and minute, but every fact　　30
Turns here to poetry, and there to prose.

Bloomfield himself is steersman : off she goes,

Cleaving the glassy flood ; blue summer smiles

Above, below ; green headlands, wooded isles

Shift past them ; and the mountain's royal folds, 35

With shadows such as purple velvet holds.

A softer landscape and a fairer sky

Around the moving boat in mirror'd beauty lie.

Bloomfield and Camlin talk, old friends and dear,

Of much ; of horses, flax-mills, home-brew'd beer ; 40

Of London ; of Ned Stanley, said to be

Lazy and *blasé* in sublime degree ;

And of elections. Laurence said, " You know,

" My rebel grandsire, sixty years ago,

" With Grattan gave his vote in College-green,   45

" Or else Lord Lisnamoy I might have been."

—" Stand for the county, Bloomfield."—" So I might.

" Under what banner would you have me fight ?"

—" They   ask'd   you ?"—" Yes,   with   watchword
        Tenant-right :

" But what had I to promise ? All my lore   50

S

" Leaves this a darker matter than before.

" Tory I'm not ; yet have no pocket plan

" To re-divide the world.   Besides, a man

" With place and solid work, had better stay

" And do what comes to hand the best he may." 55

—" You have done much."—" To make good tenants
        sure,

" And weed away the bad ; attempt a cure

" Of sloven habits, ignorance, and waste,

" (All step by step, for such things bear not haste ;)

" To teach the children ; to forbear to mix   60

" With Church affairs, or party politics—

" The simple programme, less or more fulfill'd."

—" And here you are, not ruin'd yet, nor kill'd."

—" So has it happen'd.   Still, I never saw,

" Nor yet can see, foundation for a law,   65

" Amidst our manifold complexities,

" Perplexities, (and what a web are these !)

" But here alone : waste and indebted lands

" Being wisely bought into the nation's hands,

" You might thereon create a novel class   70

" Of Irishmen, to leaven all the mass

" With hope, and industry, and loyalty,

" (My favourite crotchet—well, so let it be)

" Small Owners, namely. North, south, east, and west,

" I'd plant them, and they'd surely do their best ;   75

" With great and permanent results, if slow."

—" I wish it had been thought-of years ago !"

—" I mean to try it now, on petty scale.

" Dysart's estate was brought at last to sale

" A week since, and one good-sized lot is mine,   80

" Which, parcell'd out with care, I shall assign

" To various peasant purchasers. 'Tis plain

" Already that I shall not lose but gain

" On the mere bargain. Money must be paid,

" But part may on the land itself be laid.   85

" No burdensome conditions I inflict,

" And all on both sides shall be clear and strict."

Downing has listen'd ; his dry cautious mind

Can many doubts and difficulties find.

" Ireland and England, make the two as one."   90

—" May Heaven forfend, in case it could be done,"

Says Roe, and gently shakes his silver'd head ;

And Bloomfield, " As some measure England's thread,

" (Do nations last for ever ?) 'tis a date

" For closer partnership a day too late ! "   95

Quoth Downing, " What can Ireland singly do ?"

—" Nothing as yet : to-morrow's always new.

" Small nations to conglomerates I prefer ;

" Ireland has individual character ;

" But with her very rudiments to learn   100

" Of self-command.   Blind Fortune's wheel must turn

" In vain, till much be alter'd.   I for one,

" Save my own task, see nothing to be done."

—" No patriotism ?" says Camlin.—" Fire and sword

" In a fool's hands !   Could Ireland now afford   105

" One footplace for Astræa ?   Will our Age

" On ground like this her noblest battle wage ?

" We suffer ; pow rful England suffers too ;

" Hot writhing France has still her work to do.

" Regard the nations ; name them one by one ; 110

" More pregnant time than ours th' all-seeing Sun

" Has not beheld. But Ireland—what of her ?

" She's nothing by herself : amidst the stir

" Flung under foot or bandied to and fro,

" What comes at last ?—Our grandsons, they may
         know. 115

" Scarce worth a struggle now to re-arrange

" What's old, effete, departing,—let it change !

" I would that Irishmen could Ireland rule.

" They cannot—Irishmen are still at school ;

" Their master, England, unbelov'd 'tis true, 120

" But can we find a better one ? can you ?

" Things must (in Pistol's words) be as they may,—

" Time and the hour wear out the longest day.

" We'll do our best, because the best is best,

" (The only reason) and let slide the rest." 125

From grassy slope the Round Tower springs aloft,

With grey and orange lichen tinted soft,
Like some huge tree-trunk; its long shadow falls
Across the rough and ruin'd Abbey-walls,
And creeps o'er headstone, cross, and weedy mound,
The dial of this consecrated ground;   131
While near the shining margin of the lake,
Where crooked elder-shrubs an arbour make,
(Grotesquely stuck with many-coloured rags
By grateful devotees, as pilgrim-flags)   135
At noon its finger finds the Holy Well,
Nature's pure hermit of a rocky cell.
To this in few days more, with one consent,
Throngs of devout, of sick, of penitent,
Will come to do their prayerful pilgrimage,   140
As hath been since the good Columba's age.
" Much longer," guesses Roe; " for Pagan shrines
" Were Christianized—old bottles held new wines."
" Forms—faiths," Lord Camlin murmurs, " old and
          new?"

" See," exclaims Pictor, "how that mantle's blue 145

" Comes out against the grey-green shrubs and rocks."

" A Pilgrim surely ! " cries fair Goldylocks,

And claps her pretty cockney hands for joy.

It is indeed a woman, with a boy,

A ten-year baby, pined in face and limb,   150

Whose mother many a mile has carried him,

And now bends low in pray'r, her sick one laid

Gasping and white within the elder-shade.

" Let's go," says Bloomfield, and they turn away.

Great awe to see a human being pray   155

Had Laurence ; but in thought and word and deed

He stood aloof from every stated creed ;

Aloof, yet, if you question'd, fairly dealt,

Had thought your thoughts, had felt as you have felt,

And many men were cheer'd at inmost heart   160

That some-one dared an independent part.

The vulgar Scripture-Reader, meddling Priest,

One could not argue which he loved the least ;

Subscription-lists of theologic kind,

Whate'er their party, found him deaf and blind ; 165

No wish he harbour'd to convert the Jews,

Turks, Russians, Catholics, Chinese, Hindoos,

Cared not a pin for High Church or for Low,

Nor by what various names Dissenters go.

At last the world made up its mind to say :   170

" An odd man truly !—he must have his way,"

For thus old habitudes themselves protect,

As our own body, failing to eject,

Sheathes an intrusive particle.

                          ——" What plan

" With Irish Priests ? "—" Why, talking as a man, 175

" I say, avoid them. But a statesman might

" Have in his calculations found it right

" To yield them a less humble place at home ;

" Since now they're nothing save as part of Rome."

Bloomfield to Downing thus : and Roe agreed,— 180

" Of countries Catholic we find indeed

" Ireland most Popish ; poor and trodden-down,

" She claims the glories of the Triple Crown,

" The famous temple of Saint Peter shines,

" For head-cathedral of her humble shrines."   185

—" Ireland," said Bloomfield, " too much tends to cast

" Her thought upon the distant and the past,

" Amidst intangibilities to live,

" Her sad imagination scope to give

" In longings, in regrets, to make her boast   190

" Of fine things due or coming, fine things lost

" That once were hers, and hers would still be found

" If but the rolling world had kept its ground."

—" And yet," sigh'd Roe, " 'tis gentle heart that
          clings

" To hope's and memory's fond ideal things.   195

" Poor Erin with her harp !—This very night

" The ghosts of immemorial ages light,

" From Howth to Connemara, Donegal

" To furthest Kerry, for their festival,

" On every hill and head a mystic flame."   200

    The time of evening-conversation came

With new and various talk. A question starts
Of Meyerbeer's stage-cunning, and Mozart's,
For Jane's a good musician feminine,
A connoisseur Lord Camlin, skill'd and fine ;   205
Of Scotch and Irish music, whereof Roe
Doth more than any living mortal know ;
The modest, mild, and gravely cheerful man,
Who with the race of statisticians can
Converse as well. The 'facts' for which they care, 210
His mind will group, distinguish, blend ; as air
And light do landscapes. Now we shoot a glance
Into the heart of Poland, China, France,
America,—or aim at least ; return
To handle Ireland, yet no fingers burn.   215
Amelia thinks Pre-Raphaelites are wrong,
Complains of Robert Browning's knotty song,
And Pictor, hot in cheek, confutes the fair,
But soon forgives her for her gold-red hair.
The voice of Bloomfield—" Search the world around, 220
" Where are you safer than on Irish ground ?

" No burglar reconnoitres your abode,

" No footpad dogs you on the lonely road,

" No ruffian's arm or cowardly *garotte*,

" Walk where you please, is flung across your
        throat ;   225

" No pistol-pointing mask, with stealthy light,

" Across your slumber stoops at dead of night ;

" No friendly neighbour, spouse, or next of kin,

" Mixes your glass, to drop the powder in ;

" Confess, when you have search'd the wide world
        round,   230

" You're nowhere safer than on Irish ground.

" We Paddies, Downing, you must understand,

" Count England as a dangerous heathen land !"

—" I own, though we of Irish things complain

" Your native manners are of gentler strain.   235

" Your Scotch and English settlers still I find

" Of boorish bearing and slow stubborn mind."

—" Yet these, *per contra*," Bloomfield must admit,

" Are loyal, truthful, though of sluggish wit.

" I like them, sturdy, sulky, jealous tribe,   240

" Though to their Orange Hall I can't subscribe.

—" And Ribbonism?"—" How much I used to hear

" Of Ribbonism, the landlord's hourly fear!"

—" And you have quell'd it—'twas a noble task!"

—" I know not if I have; I never ask.   245

" It sometimes said, *Take Notice*, I took none,

" And what we plann'd was resolutely done;

" My own folk saw me willing to be just

" And something more; I told them, 'I intrust

" ' My life to you.' When any lost his land,   250

" 'Twas mildly managed; all could understand

" The need; and so on."—" Would you not be loth

" To trust a man who took the Ribbon oath?"

—" Men's lives, and human character, are such,

" Perhaps it puzzles most to know too much;   255

" I ask no questions."

              No: but Laurence knew

Some things unsought, as frank men always do.

Whilst yet his reign was but a few weeks old,

The Doran's lifelong heartburn he consoled
With much-desiderated lease, and more   260
Of moorland joined to what they had before.
Warmly towards their youthful king they felt,
Who also his especial favour dealt
To Neal, but knew not what a burden lay
On the boy's mind.   Neal told the truth one day. 265
" A Ribbonman am I,—send me to jail,
" Or where you will, sir."   Laurence heard his tale,
And sent him round by Ailsa Craig, to watch
Awhile how Sandy farms, and learn broad Scotch.
Much happens in a year.   A spy betray'd   270
The poteen-still, and by the heels was laid
The cunning Connaughtman, who in his turn,
Enraged and ruin'd, thought it well to earn
The public money, not indeed for blood,
He could not prove enough ; but much he could, 275
Which sent Tim Nulty, and five other men,
To fifteen years of punishment, and ten,
And broke the Lodge in pieces, with dismay

And heavy dread, not passing soon away.

First Bloomfield's folk, then nearly all the rest,   280

At 'God's Tribunal' now their sin confess'd,

And from their oath absolved, with penance due,

Felt thankful great relief, and started new ;

Some, if not all, upon a wiser course.

Of these was Denis ; who with generous force   285

His gratitude to generous Laurence gave,

And Laurence liked the sturdy man and brave,

Steadfast to Bridget, made at last his wife

When Neal return'd to prop the old folks' life.

Since Laurence built his Inn, the bustling pair   290

With honest pride are host and hostess there,—

Small show, much comfort, and each liquor's name

The one it has authentic right to claim ;

No vitriolic whiskey, fit to sear

Your vitals up, no sour malignant beer.   295

Poor Paddy of all Christian men I think

On basest food pours down the vilest drink ;

'God's Tribunal,' the confessional.

But not in Bloomfield's kingdom ; long did Jane
Endeavour, and at last not all in vain,
That wives and daughters should know how to
      cook.   300
Upwards, they both say, bid the humbler look ;
Appropriate wishes breed not discontent ;
For strength's renewal petty hopes are lent ;
So live we, so improve. A tidy cottage,
Garb of stout homespun, mess of savoury pottage, 305
Such grows the fashion ; him that duly tries
His Honour helps with all goodwill to rise.
" And what then," Downing ask'd, " is Ribbonism ?"
—" A morbid sign, a proof of social schism.
" No one can tell you is it widely spread ;   310
" All tails I guess it, and without a head ;
" A sort of stinging zoophite, that breeds
' " In rotten places, and from vagrant seeds."
—" Well, comfort and contentment hand in hand
" Grow strong or feeble over every land :   315
" And your folk are contented ?"—" Why, so far

" As Sons of Erin may, perhaps they are.

" But common evils which to life belong

" Patricius will account a personal wrong ;

" Suckled on grievances, his mind is bent   320

" To charge on others all his discontent ;

" Half curses England when his tooth-ache stings,

" Half blames th' Established Church for frosty springs

" And rainy summers ; thinks it passing hard

" From any joy of life to live debarr'd,   325

" As though the English, French, or German poor

" Lead plenteous lives, with nothing to endure."

—" What's this !" said Jane ; " O yes they are, I'm sure,

" Contented."—" Well, perhaps they are, my dear ;

" As much as may be ; yet I always hear   330

" The human discontent in murmuring motion

" Round every limit, like the murmuring ocean.

" Come, let us go. The bonfires are alight.

" I'll hold you safe from Captain Rock to-night.

" Now, Miss Amelia ;—"

                      From the fir-grove mound   335

They view the shadowy country, leagues around,
Spotted with fires ; upon the mountain ridge
One like a rising star ; and one a bridge
Of quivering gold across the dusky lake ;
Successive torches, like a fiery snake, 340
Wind creeping through the foliage, in and out,
With black figures athwart, whose muffled shout
Hurts not the whispering airs that come and go
Among the fir-boughs and warm grass below.
Now by sweet-scented path they take their way 345
Between the dusky swathes of new-mown hay,
Down to the cross-roads' patch, enclosed with trees
And flower-girt walls of peeping cottages,
To find the nearest Bonfire—crumbled wide
In glowing ruins, and on every side 350
The women snatching ruddy coals, for fear
Their hearth should miss good luck throughout the year.
But quickly now approach, with clamorous noise,
The torches, in a mob of men and boys,
Who draw to Bloomfield's gazing group, extend 355

T

The loose array to left and right, and bend
All round them, not too closely, in a ring,
From which the huge reed-flambeaux towering fling
Wild flare upon the crowd, with shadows wild,
And on the trees' dark wall above them piled.   360
Amelia shrinks to Jane's courageous arm,
Who smiles away her pretty friend's alarm.
Forth steps a torch-man.   "Hats off, boys! be ready!
" God bless his Honour, and his darlin' Lady!—
" God bless the two fine childre', that's not here!— 365
" *Cead millia faltia*, noble guests!"—a cheer
Thrice o'er the glimmering lake swells out and dies.
Faint echo from the mountain-land replies.

Gaze from the Hall: the fires are well-nigh dead,
But in the clear dark summer vault o'erhead   370
A mild three-quarter moon and stars a few
Burn quenchless, and the heav'n is lighted through
With faintest daylight, whereof none can say

Cead millia faltia, a hundred thousand welcomes.

Iᴛ that it be the old or newborn day.

Alas ! the year has touched its height of hope,   375

And lessening day on day begin to slope

To gloomy winter. All, we know, must die :

But when we feel it, who forbears to sigh ?—

To bed, to bed ! amidst the doubtful gleam ;

And mingle Past and Future in a dream.   380

Says Downing, brought by Bloomfield round the land

Next morning,—" Now at last I understand.

" I knew your liberal notions, never knew

" How you contrived to raise your rental too.

" I see you have, as groundwork, study made,   385

" Close, persevering, of the farmer's trade.

" Hard work, no doubt, at first."

                            " Plans fail'd, beside,

" And many cheated, more to cheat me tried ;

" All has work'd round by slow and sure degrees,

" To something doubtless,—but one never sees   390

" His hope come true ; in daylight disappear

" The vision's glories. . . . Let me show you here

" A solid thing enough.   Seven years ago

" With gorse above, and plashy bog below,

" This was a dreary wilderness and wide,   395

" With one poor cottage on the moorland-side.

" Twelve little households now possess a place,

" And each the centre of a widening space

" Of useful ground.   Besides their work at home,

" The men and youths to farming labour come   400

" In Spring or Harvest on the neighbouring lands,

" But not as once, with slavish hungry hands,

" Toiling for husks, and as they toil'd the more,

" More helpless, pinch'd, and poorer than before."

—" Wages are higher ?"—" Yes, I gladly say,   405

" And far more work too finish'd in a day.

" Every day-labourer, if worthy found,

" Ere long obtains a cheap small bit of ground ;

" Help with a house ; with more ambitious eyes,

" May look to win a waste-plot if he tries ;   410

" But first probationary powers must show,

" And on the list with all his rivals go.

" There should be, as the soldiers have in France,

" In humblest work an opening to advance.

" Best government gives every man his chance.   415

" That's justice,—but still more the weak may claim,

" And merely justice in the strong were blame."

" This house is Doran's, who was pioneer

" Amid the waste, and lived in constant fear

" Of those above him. He and his at length   420

" To other shores had turn'd their heart and strength :

" But here remain the old man and his wife,

" A healthy couple still, of easy life.

" A year ago their son, so things befell,

" Essay'd my stewardship, and does it well.   425

" Their daughter, married, lives at Lisnamoy,

" Fair hostess of the Inn ; her six-year boy

" Lives mainly with the old folk, who employ

" A sturdy youth's assistance for their land,

" And keep their place, you see, with tidy hand."   430

Trim on its farm the little mansion stood,

Amidst, e'en yet, a seeming solitude

Of craggy hills above, brown bog below.

Cheap all-enriching ivy (sure to grow

Where Bloomfield's likings are a law of love)   435

Clasping the gable, show'd its sprays above

White wall and well-kept thatch ; field, fence, and
     lane,

Once vile as beggar's garb, now carried plain

The look of thrift and hopeful industry,

Proud, not ashamed, to toil successfully.   440

A regiment of young trees stood well in rank,

To guard from swooping gale an open flank,

And here and there, with due entrenchment round,

Green larches held the rugged bits of ground.

They entered : rows of dish and cup shone bright 445

Along the dresser ; and a warm delight

Made Maureen's good old face more shining still

As Bloomfield shook her hand with right good-will ;

While grandson Johnny timidly must creep

And sidle off, and round a corner peep.   450
Would they sit down ?—And, oh it was too much,
But could their Honours any one thing touch ?
" Your *bunya-rowa* to my friend I've praised,"
And each the milky bowl rejoicing raised.
They saw the garden, with its homely space   455
Of onions, parsley, cabbage, catching grace
From bordering marigolds, high hollyhocks,
Tufted queen-daisies ; under mossy rocks
Stood beehives ranged along its upper end,
And willows to a bow'r were taught to bend ;   460
Then passing to the door were met by Jack,
A sturdy toiler still, though bow'd in back,
Who show'd his fields and methods, old and new,
Yet with a lingering touch of caution too.
With humble cough he prefaced each reply,   465
And glanced at Downing with suspicious eye.

Next to Neal Doran's house, in central site,

bunya-rowa, thick milk.

Warm brick emboss'd with roses red and white.
His wife, a comely, smiling little dame,
Was busy with her baby when they came ;   470
And soon arrived the Steward, young and stout,
With face of active boldness looking out
Through calm intelligence; his words but few,
Respectful, grave, and confidential too.
Master and servant lived in mutual trust.   475
How sweet is life when men are kind and just !
" A fortnight hence we go, Neal,—must prepare,"—
And so they talked of this and that affair.

The guests are gone. Midsummer time is past.
Laurence and Jane a longing wish have cast   480
To Thor and Odin's land, resolved to see
(Bold travellers they in many a far countrie)
The rough and jagged edge of Europe, where
White Sulitelma looks through purest air
Over pine-forests, cataracts, deep still fiords;   485
And Gulbrandsdal hath for its peasant-lords

Maintain'd their old inheritances; each
Warm in his fir-built palace, out of reach
Of winter and the wolf, on those long nights
That arch the waste of snow with mystic lights. 490
A country poor and perilous; yet kind,
As *Gamle Norge's* grateful children find.

Mary and Fred to Jane's good sister go,
In Dublin; one whose marriage fails to know
The joy of blest maternity, but scant   495
In no good office that becomes an aunt.
Sir Ulick's house the children seldom see;
Infirm in body and in mind is he;
My Lady Harvey, as a woman can,
Makes wretched all around her. On her plan   500
One daughter's married; one remains to fret;
Richard, her eldest son and former pet,
Has mingled wormwood in her bowl of life
By choosing for himself a charming wife.
Dick, when he comes, of Bloomfield's talk is fain, 505

And Mary Harvey bosom-friends with Jane.
Meanwhile the old *régime* creaks lumbering on,—
A crawling flattering creature, hight Malone,
Once clerk to Pigot, now for agent placed;
Some think a cheat, and sure to be disgraced.　510

Sir Ulick's younger daughter, so they say,
Was jilted by Lord Crashton—well-a-day!
I mean the young Lord, when the old Lord died.
He to the last on Satan loudly cried,
And cursed his only son with parting breath,　515
A son right joyful of his father's death.
The young Lord's ways 'tis wisdom not to know;
The firm in Dublin, meanwhile, smoothly go
From year to year with all his bonds and lands,
Which rest completely in their skilful hands;　520
And Phinn and Wedgely well their secrets keep.
A slice is theirs of every ox and sheep,
Or, some think, lion's share.　For good or harm,
This broad estate is one huge grazing farm.

How fare the other neighbours of our Squire ? 525
Dysart, sold up, to Dublin will retire,
And live there, Heaven, or else the Deuce, knows how.
O'Hara died at Rome : trustees have now
His large bequest, to found a nunnery,
And college, when convenient; squeezing dry   530
The land and tenants meanwhile. Finlay, cold
And hard at all times, now is too-too old,
Is turn'd a very walking icicle,
From which no sun or fire can coax one rill,
One drop of kindness. With his silent spouse   535
And cloddish sons he keeps a dismal house,
Bargains at every fair, and has not thought
How he is with his cattle sold and bought.
Tough Isaac Brown, because the times grew bad,
Much conflict with his petty tenants had,   540
And, beef and mutton rising every day,
Drove men and women by the score away ;
Some on the Union (his Division) came,
Which vex'd him. Twice his rick-yard roar'd in flame.

He thinks assassins on his footsteps wait,   545
And four policemen live beside his gate.
His wife, long-lingering, dead, this tough old Brown
Soon made a young and florid lass his own;
And for the purse-strings they have many a fight.
His son enlisted; daughter Nell took flight   550
With stolen money, and a labouring lad.
Old Isaac's temper now is bitter-bad;
Ghoul-greedy grows his appetite for gain;
Some think him softening, not in heart but brain.

 Has Bloomfield mov'd these men? Small sign
   appears.   555
They learn but little from the days and years.
" I thought," said he to Jane, " that by degrees
" Persuasive reason would have wrought on these
" To join for some good ends : with what disgust,
" What rage they always listen, if they must,   560
" To mere proposals for the general good !
" A stupid rich man's gross tyrannic mood

" Enrages one in turn, and goads to fight,

" And some wrong things have thus been twisted
       right

" With weary work. What pleasure (here's reward) 565

" In one's own limits to make some accord

" Of wish and fact, with aidance always near

" From speckless mind and loving heart, most dear ! ...

" How little can be done, my Jane, at best !—

" The landscape here is noble; shall we rest ?" 570

Thus on Croghmore said Laurence, just a day

Before they started on their northern way.

Two mountain ponies bore them up as far

As that grey limestone crag, with rift and scar,

Which keeps the summit like a castle-wall, 575

Titanic, dreadful. Sunshine over all

The world was spread, and on a knoll or crown

Warm-scented with wild thyme, these two sat down.

   The verdant mountain slopes from stair to stair ;

A cottage whitely nestling here and there ; 580

Atop stands built the dizzy limestone ledge ;

Below, smooth curves embrace the water's edge,

And round the clear lough, gemm'd with islands green,

Rise lower crags, with darkling glens between,

Thick-grown with nut and fern and rowan-spray, 585

Through which the falling streamlets find their way.

Far-distant, clothed in soft aerial blue,

A peaky summit bounds the wider view,

A brother mountain, swept by ocean-gales,

Where fishers' roofs are hid in wider vales ;   590

Mountain to mountain looks, as king to king,

And embassies of clouds high message bring ;

Great thunders roll between, when storm-eclipse

Shuts either landmark from arriving ships ;

The starry dome suspended high aloof   595

Bows on these pillars its perennial roof.

But now, bright sunshine broods upon the world,

With silence ; save the boom of bee uncurl'd

From bed of thyme ; or when a marvellous thing,

Horns, beard, and yellow eyes, with sudden spring 600

Cresting some fragment like a hippogriff,
Is gone, its goat-bleat echoing from the cliff.

They see the lake and islands mapp'd below,
Through broad green plains the river's glittering flow,
Partition'd farms, and roofs where men abide,   605
The Town's light smoke, on grovy hill descried ;
Corn-fields and meadows, rocky mounts they see,
Dale, sheep-walk, moorland, bog, and grassy lea;
But all, from mountain-skirts to distant coast,
In one expanse and one impression lost ;   610
A wavy ten-league landscape, light and large,
Lonely and sad, on Europe's furthest marge.
" ' A plenteous place of hospitable cheer
" ' Is Holy Ireland !'—often did I hear
" That song in Gaelic from my nurse.   Poor land ! 615
" ' There's honey where her misty vales expand.'
" Her sons and daughters love her; yet they fly
" As from a city of the plague; and why ?—
" Poor Madge herself, when I was still a boy,

" Sail'd westward, beyond search : at Lisnamoy   620

" I could not find one creature of her race.

" The people flee by myriads, and their place

" Knows them no more.   On whom or what to blame

" We disagree, and struggle without aim.

" Some wish us joy; we're losers all the same.   625

" Yet would I merely stop the current ?   No.

" How many I myself have help'd to go.

" 'Tis best for them—and sad it should be so."

—" But, Laurence, you in this desponding mood !

" Who've done your land and people so much good,—

" In joy of work accomplish'd,—on this eve   631

" Of happy holiday ! "—

                         " 'Tis sad to leave

" One's home, on gayest journey : Shall we find

" Again the very things we've left behind ? . . .

" But past our bounds my thought o'er Ireland flew,

" And only saw a dreary dismal view.   636

" This mild green country in the western sea,

" With guardian mountains, rivers full and free,

" Home of a brave, rich-brain'd, warm-hearted race,—
" This Ireland should have been a noble place   640

   " It will be," Jane replied.

                      And so they left
Their purple couch, and clomb a rocky cleft,
Steep, narrow, known to mountaineers, and stood
On the bare summit,—kingly solitude,
Apart, yet public to the earth and sky.   645
Drunken with bliss, the proud exulting eye
Swept o'er the billowy hills, cloud-shadow'd, roll'd
Like spotted sultan-serpent, fold on fold ;
Faint violet valleys; specks of burning gold
On brook or tarn; a world below spread fine   650
Of delicate rainbows, to the far-off shine
Intense but dim of Ocean, like Heaven's gate ;
All over-canopied with pomp and state
Of clouds, pure gulfs, and glowing light profound
Wherewith the Sun o'erflow'd th' horizon round.   655

Their bosoms with a wordless rapture swell'd,

Gazing upon these glories.   Laurence held

The wifely hand, with little ring wherethro'

Her life-stream coursed in wandering veins of blue,

And press'd it to his lips with perfect love.

A psalm was in their souls to GOD above.   660

Earth, ocean, spreading round them, and on high

The regions of the everlasting sky.

FINIS.

R. CLAY, SON, AND TAYLOR, PRINTERS, LONDON.

The List of Titles
in the Garland Series

MARIA EDGEWORTH

1. Castle Rackrent *(1800)*

2. An Essay on Irish Bulls *(1802)*

3. Ennui *(1809)*

4. The Absentee *(1812)*

5. Ormond *(1817)*

SYDNEY OWENSON, LADY MORGAN

6. The Wild Irish Girl *(1806)*

7. O'Donnel. A National Tale *(1814)*

8. Florence Macarthy: an Irish Tale *(1818)*

9. The O'Briens and the O'Flahertys *(1817)*

10. Dramatic Sketches from Real Life *(1833)*

CHARLES ROBERT MATURIN

11. The Wild Irish Boy *(1808)*

12. The Milesian Chief *(1812)*

13. Women; or, Pour et Contre: A Tale *(1818)*

EYRE EVANS CROWE

14. To-day in Ireland *(1825)*

15. Yesterday in Ireland *(1829)*

JOHN BANIM AND MICHAEL BANIM

16. Tales, by the O'Hara Family *(1825)*

17. The Boyne Water, A Tale, by the O'Hara Family *(1826)*

18. Tales, by the O'Hara Family. Second Series *(1826)*

19. The Croppy. A Tale of 1798 *(1828)*

20. The Anglo-Irish of the Nineteenth Century *(1828)*

21. The Denounced *(1830)*

22. The Ghost-Hunter and his Family *(1833)*

23. The Mayor of Wind-Gap *and* Canvassing *(1835)*

24. The Bit O'Writin' and Other Tales *(1838)*

25. PATRICK JOSEPH MURRAY, The Life of John Banim, the Irish Novelist *(1857)*

GERALD GRIFFIN

26. Holland-Tide; or, Munster Popular Tales *(1827)*

27. Tales of the Munster Festivals *(1827)*

28. The Collegians *(1829)*

29. The Rivals *and* Tracy's Ambition *(1829)*

30. Tales of My Neighbourhood *(1835)*

31. Talis Qualis; or Tales of the Jury Room *(1842)*

32. DANIEL GRIFFIN, The Life of Gerald Griffin by his Brother, revised edition *(n.d.)*

WILLIAM CARLETON

33. Father Butler. The Lough Dearg Pilgrim *(1829)*

34. Traits and Stories of the Irish Peasantry *(1830)*

35. Traits and Stories of the Irish Peasantry, Second Series *(1833)*

36. Tales of Ireland *(1834)*

37. Fardorougha, the Miser; or, the Convicts of Lisnamona *(1839)*

38. The Fawn of Spring-Vale, The Clarionet, and Other Tales *(1841)*

39. Tales and Sketches Illustrating the Character of the Irish Peasantry *(1845)*

40. Valentine M'Clutchy, The Irish Agent; or, Chronicles of the Castle Cumber Property *(1847)*

41. The Black Prophet: a Tale of the Irish Famine *(1847)*

42. The Emigrants of Ahadarra: A Tale of Irish Life *(1848)*

43. The Tithe Proctor: being a Tale of the Tithe
    Rebellion in Ireland *(1849)*

44. The Life of William Carleton: Being His
    Autobiography and Letters; and an Account of his
    Life and Writings from the Point at which the
    Autobiography Breaks Off by David O'Donoghue
    (1896)

HARRIET MARTINEAU

45. Ireland *(1832)*

ANNA MARIA HALL

46. Sketches of Irish Character *(1829)*

47. Lights and Shadows of Irish Life *(1838)*

48. The Whiteboy. A Story of Ireland in 1822 *(1845)*

49. Stories of the Irish Peasantry *(1851)*

WILLIAM HAMILTON MAXWELL

50. O'Hara; or 1798 *(1825)*

51. The Fortunes of Hector O'Halloran and his man,
    Mark Anthony O'Toole *(1843)*

52. Erin-Go-Bragh; or Irish Life Pictures *(1859)*

ANTHONY TROLLOPE

53. The Macdermots of Ballycloran *(1847)*

54. The Kellys and the O'Kellys *(1848)*

55. Castle Richmond *(1860)*

56. An Eye for an Eye *(1879)*

57. The Land-Leaguers *(1883)*

JOSEPH SHERIDAN LE FANU

58. The Purcell Papers with a Memoir by Alfred
    Perceval Graves *(1880)*

59. The Cock and Anchor: Being a Chronicle of Old
    Dublin City *(1845)*

60. The House by the Church-Yard *(1863)*

WILLIAM ALLINGHAM

61. Lawrence Bloomfield in Ireland. A Modern Poem
    (1864)

CHARLOTTE RIDDELL (MRS. J.H. RIDDELL)

62. Maxwell Drewitt *(1865)*

63. The Nun's Curse *(1888)*

T. MASON JONES

64. Old Trinity. A Story of Real Life *(1867)*

ANNIE KEARY

65. Castle Daly. The Story of an Irish Home Thirty
    Years Ago *(1875)*

MAY LAFFAN HARTLEY

66. Hogan, M. P. *(1876)*

67. Flitters, Tatters, and the Counsellor and Other
    Sketches *(1879)*

CHARLES JOSEPH KICKHAM

68. Knocknagow: or, the Cabins of Tipperary *(1879)*

MARGARET M. BREW

69. The Burtons of Dunroe *(1880)*

70. Chronicles of Castle Cloyne. Pictures of Munster
    Life *(1885)*

EMILY LAWLESS

71. Hurrish. A Study *(1886)*

72. With Essex in Ireland *(1890)*

73. Grania. The Story of an Island *(1892)*

74. Maelcho. A Sixteenth-Century Narrative *(1894)*

75. Traits and Confidences *(1898)*

WILLIAM O'BRIEN

76. When We Were Boys *(1890)*

ANONYMOUS

77. Priests and People: A No-Rent Romance *(1891)*